MW01690889

Grade 5 | Unit 8

Native Americans
A Changing Landscape

Reader

Amplify Core Knowledge Language Arts

Core Knowledge®

ISBN: 978-1-68161-216-4

Printed in the USA
07 LSCOW 2021

Contents

Native Americans

A Changing Landscape

Reader

"If we ever owned the land, we own it still, for we never sold it..."

Chief Joseph-Nez Perce

Chapter 1

A Long and Winding Road

THE BIG QUESTION
How did European exploration and settlement of what is now the United States change the way Native Americans lived?

Imagine you were born three hundred years ago on America's Great Plains. Back then, there were no big cities or highways. The landscape reveals only wide-open prairies with rolling hills, lazy rivers, and endless grassland.

Imagine the prairie is your home. Perhaps you are a young Sioux. This is where you were born, and you already know that you will live here all your life. Everything you need to survive is here, amid the grasses and low, rolling hills. Food, shelter, clothing, water, fire, friends, family, and sacred places—everything is here for you.

However, even if the prairie contains everything you need to survive, where on the grassy plains do you find food? What do you use to build a house or make a fire? Where do you find water? How can you survive the frigid, icy winters and the scorching summers?

The answers to these questions are easy to find, as long as you are willing to learn from those who came before you. The people, your people, have been here for some 10,000 years or more. The wisdom and stories of hundreds of generations is your ***birthright****—the most precious thing you will ever own.*

The elders tell you stories. They teach you about your place in the world, and they provide the wisdom that is passed down from one generation to another. Your ancestors were the first to walk this land, and they learned to survive here with only their brains, muscles, and courage to ***sustain*** *them. They were the first to hear the winds and see the waving grass. They found the rivers. You believe their spirits are in the hills and grassy plains, and in the soil beneath your feet.*

Most importantly, your ancestors learned to track and hunt the buffalo. The buffalo provide food, shelter, clothing, fuel for fires, and tools. Out here on the Great Plains, your tribe and all the tribes of the Great Plains depend on the buffalo for survival.

American Buffalo (bison) on plain

The tribes of the Great Plains are certainly not alone in the Americas. There are others, and if you walk far enough in any direction, you will find them. North, south, east, or west, there are different tribes in every habitable place. Over thousands of years, they have learned to survive.

Native American tribes lived in every habitable place.

In the southwest, you will meet the Navajo, Pueblo, and all the other tribes of the canyons and deserts. Head southeast and you will find the Cherokee, Creek, and Seminole thriving in the humid woods and swamplands. In the dense, chilly forests to the northeast, there are the Huron and the Six Nations of the great Iroquois Confederacy. To the west, on the dry, flat plateau between the snowy peaks of the Teton and Cascade Mountains, you will meet Shoshone and Nez Perce. Farther west, where trees grow as tall as mountains, you may meet the Chinook, the Pomo, and all the other tribes nestled along the western coast.

Some of the people you meet will be your friends. You will share stories and you will trade with them. Some of them will be your enemies, just as they were enemies to your grandparents and great-grandparents, and they will want to fight. This is the way it has always been, and so you will need to be prepared if you travel from your homeland.

If you are like most Native Americans living on the Great Plains, you will find that you are quite happy to stay and live with your family and friends, the members of your tribe. You do not need to wander too far from home. You will live here on the plains forever, tracking and hunting the buffalo, raising children of your own and teaching them how to live according to the ways of your ancestors. Life is just fine here on the plains. You have everything you need, and little changes, until it does…

Exploration and Settlement

The year 1492 CE is a notable date in history—especially American history. Christopher Columbus sailed from Spain in that year to look for a passage to Asia, because that is what he thought he would find across the Atlantic Ocean. Instead, he bumped into a new continent. Columbus's voyage triggered what some call an Age of Discovery. He was just one of many, many explorers from Spain, England, France, and other European countries to travel across the Atlantic.

At first, the Europeans did not know what to call this land. Some called it the West Indies, because they thought it was part of Asia. Later, they named it the Americas, after an Italian explorer named Amerigo Vespucci who figured out it really was a new continent—or, more precisely, two new continents: North and South America. Many Europeans simply referred to it as the New World because it was not on any of their maps, and everything seemed strange and new to them. For Europeans, this New World promised not only new lands but also incredible riches: gold, silver, sugar, tobacco, lumber, animal furs, and a host of other resources. European nations sent armies to fight over these riches, and they sent settlers to harvest them.

As you probably know, Columbus was not the first person to find the Americas. European explorers and settlers encountered people everywhere they went. These were the original or "native" people of the Americas because they had lived on this land before anyone else. Some Europeans called them Indians, although they were not really in the Indies at all. The name stuck, and that is why you hear the term *American Indian* today.

Beginning in 1492 CE, many things began to change for the **indigenous** peoples of North and South America. For some, the change came quickly. This was especially true in places such as Mexico and Peru, where the Aztec and Inca empires ruled. Their civilizations fell quickly to Spanish conquerors. The Spanish brought their powerful guns, steel swords, and horses. They (and all other Europeans) also brought diseases against which the native peoples had no natural defenses. By the end of the 1500s, Spanish soldiers and diseases wiped out many groups of people from Mexico through South America.

Change was more gradual for Native Americans in the part of North America that later became the United States. Although the early Spanish explorers built several settlements north of Mexico, they did not conquer all of this land. However, the Spanish were not the only Europeans interested in the Americas. The English, French, Portuguese, and Dutch also crossed the ocean in search of riches. They, too, sent explorers, and soon they built settlements and colonies of their own.

The English settled at Jamestown, Virginia, where they built a fort in 1607 CE. There, Captain John Smith met Pocahontas and her tribe, the Powhatan. A few years later, in 1620 CE, the Pilgrims landed at Plymouth Rock. They interacted with the Wampanoag people, including a man named Tisquantum, also known as Squanto, who helped them learn to survive. The Pilgrims were grateful to Squanto for his help. According to some historical records, the Pilgrims and Native Americans came together for a meal to share the bounty of their harvest. Today we remember and celebrate this meal as Thanksgiving.

As with the story of Columbus, the story of Thanksgiving is only a fragment of a much larger story about Native Americans and the impact Europeans had on their world. Unfortunately, the themes of the Thanksgiving story—such as cooperation, friendship, and gratitude—are not common in the history of relations between Native Americans and Europeans.

A Changing World: East and West

If you were a Native American boy or girl born somewhere on the Great Plains during the 1500s or 1600s, European explorers existed mainly in rumors and campfire tales. In other words, most Plains tribes did not meet many Europeans at first, but they probably did hear stories about them. Where did these stories come from?

Native Americans usually traded with neighboring tribes. Each tribe had something that another tribe needed. They traded animal furs, plants and herbs, pottery, jewelry, and tools or weapons made from various stones, bones, wood, or shells. Whenever they traded things, they also talked and shared news and stories that they heard from other tribes. Around the fire at night, they shared stories of strange men from distant lands. Some said these men came from the sea itself, while others told of giant sailing ships. These strange men had beards, and they wore metal armor on their bodies. They carried powerful weapons that made the sound of thunder echo through the forests and canyons. They also rode on great beasts called horses. Native Americans had never seen any of these things before Europeans arrived.

Native Americans trading with each other

On the other hand, change was somewhat swifter for tribes in the East. From Florida all the way up to Maine and Canada, ships carrying eager and adventurous Europeans arrived. They came from England, France, Spain, the Netherlands, and other countries. They did not come simply to explore the land, hunt for valuable furs, and take treasure back to their homes in the so-called Old World, they came to stay. For eastern tribes, life became very challenging as Europeans moved in and established farms, towns, and cities.

Europeans trading with Native Americans

European settlers were interested in two things even more valuable than furs. First, they needed knowledge to aid their survival, which Native Americans had in great supply. Native Americans showed settlers how to grow native plants like corn, beans, and tobacco. They taught them where to hunt for their own beaver, bear, and buffalo hides. They taught them the secrets of the forests and mountains and rivers. They also taught them about other tribes.

Second, settlers wanted land. English settlers established 13 colonies on the East Coast. Over time, the Native American tribes in these areas lost most of their land or were forced to move to **reservations** as European settlers built farms, roads, towns, factories, and cities. Gradually, the settlers ventured away from the East Coast and over the Appalachian Mountains. They encountered the vast landscape of the American West. To them, it must have seemed like a land of opportunity, as such expansion and settlement was no longer possible in Europe.

In 1776, those 13 colonies became the United States, and its government had a plan to make the new nation strong and powerful. The U.S. government seized land where Native American tribes lived. Many tribes fought back, but they could not prevent their land from being taken. The Cherokee people, for example, were one of the last large, powerful tribes in the woodlands of the southeastern United States. As the United States expanded its reach during the early 1800s, more and more settlers moved onto Cherokee lands, creating **tensions** that boiled over into war. The Cherokee tried to adapt to life as farmers and live according to the laws of the United States. Ultimately, though, the U.S. government (under President Andrew Jackson) decided there was no room for the Cherokee or any other tribes. With the Indian Removal Act of 1830, the Cherokee and other tribes east of the Mississippi River were forced to move west to newly established "Indian Territory," in what would later become Oklahoma. Thousands of Cherokee and other Native Americans died on the long walk westward, a journey remembered today as the Trail of Tears.

The Cherokee experience—including the tension, wars, and **forced relocation** to reservation land—was a narrative that played out again and again with other Native American tribes during the 1800s. Eventually, most tribes in the present-day United States, including the tribes of the Great Plains, experienced a similar fate. As you will learn, there are many sad, tragic chapters in the Native American story. The Native American way of life—which had existed for thousands of years before Europeans arrived—was seriously threatened. Fortunately, however, Native American cultures did not vanish. Although it was not easy, many Native American tribes did survive and redefined themselves to become part of a new nation, the United States. Their age-old traditions are still celebrated, and they still walk upon the land they love.

Horses

The Spanish brought many horses from Europe. They traded some horses to Native Americans, but many more simply escaped into the wild. Native Americans learned to train and ride horses. Horses eventually transformed a way of life for many tribes. This was especially true on the Great Plains, where horses made hunting, traveling, and fighting much easier.

Forced relocation of the Cherokee

Chapter 2

Across Mountains and Prairies

THE BIG QUESTION
How did European ideas of land ownership conflict with the beliefs and cultures of Native American tribes living in the Great Plains, Great Basin, and Northwest Plateau?

Before America was divided into colonies and eventually states, there were no borders, fences, or **property lines**. The only boundaries were those set by nature: wide rivers, deep canyons, parched deserts, high mountains, and dense forests. Early European explorers and settlers stayed mostly in the eastern portions of what would one day become the United States of America. The English established their colonies along the East Coast, and the French settled in parts of Canada and the Louisiana Territory. When the United States gained independence in 1776, and for many years afterward, few Europeans really knew what lay beyond the Ohio River Valley. Few European explorers had ever crossed the Mississippi River. Although people knew about California because the Spanish had settlements there, what lay west of the Mississippi River was a mystery to those living on the East Coast.

As many people of the United States would learn—thanks to explorers such as Meriwether Lewis and William Clark—the grassy prairies of the Great Plains extend more than a thousand miles west of the Mississippi River. Then, the Rocky Mountains appear, their jagged, snowy peaks rising over 14,000 feet straight up into the clouds. Cross those mountains and travel due west, and you will descend into the sands of the Great Basin. Or, farther north between the Rockies and the gorgeous Cascade Mountain Range, discover the canyons and pine-shrub forests of the Northwest Plateau.

Combined, these three regions—the Great Plains, Great Basin, and the Northwest Plateau—cover nearly one million square miles, or about one-third of the continental United States. In the early 1800s, these three regions were home to hundreds of different Native American tribes. By that time, the tribes in the East, including the Cherokee and many others, had already suffered disease, war, and forced relocation. There were still Native Americans in the East, but for the most part they were absorbed into the society and laws of the United States.

Out West, however, on the Great Plains and beyond, most people still lived according to their ancient **customs**. None of those tribes claimed to own any of the land they lived on, not in the sense that it was theirs to sell or buy. They did not have **property deeds** or titles. Each tribe did have an area they called home, and the people worked together and shared the fruits of the land. This was the land of their ancestors. It was the land where all their people were born and died. It was their belief that the people could not own the land because they were part of the land, just like the plants and animals. Eventually, this viewpoint—that people were caretakers rather than owners of the land—added to tension and mistrust between Native Americans and settlers from the United States and other nations. The lack of defined borders and property lines made it easy for outsiders to claim land and force Native Americans to move. The settlers carried deeds, or papers, claiming that the land was theirs. The Native Americans had no such papers.

Traditional Ways

On the Great Plains and beyond, each tribe knew exactly how far they could go before they met a neighboring tribe, and they knew whether that tribe was friend or foe. Whether they were friends or enemies, they held this same respect for all the living things on the land and in the sky and water, including the animals they killed for food. They saw that all living things were part of the same earth, sharing the same soil and air. They believed everything came from the same creator, even if each tribe called that creator by a different name.

Children learned their history through fireside stories and singing the songs of their ancestors. They learned to use the earth's gifts through daily chores, gathering food, tending to crops, and hunting. They also learned about their religion by participating in rituals and ceremonies. There were ceremonies to mark the changing of the seasons, births, deaths, marriages, and coming-of-age events, such as a child's first kill while hunting.

Ceremonies brought people together. There was singing, dancing, drumming, special costumes and foods, and a wide variety of rituals. But these events were not simply for entertainment. These were sacred ceremonies.

Ceremonies have always been an important part of Native American cultures.

Sharing to Survive

An author named Mourning Dove (1888–1936), from the Okanagan tribe in the Plateau region, wrote of one basic ritual that helped young girls learn important lessons about their role within the tribe:

Children were encouraged to develop strict discipline and a high regard for sharing. When a girl picked her first berries and dug her first roots, they were given away to an elder so she would share her future success. When a child carried water for the home, an elder would give compliments, pretending to taste meat in water carried by a boy, or berries in that of a girl. The child was encouraged not to be lazy and to grow straight like a sapling.

Simple rituals such as these taught children what it truly meant to be part of the tribe. They learned that sharing was not simply a matter of kindness, it was a matter of survival.

Vision Quest

In many tribes throughout the Great Plains and other regions, older boys—and sometimes girls—were expected to participate in a **Vision Quest**. This coming-of-age ceremony marked a young person's **transition** to adulthood. During a Vision Quest, a young person, or quester, sought to understand his purpose in life.

The most important part of a vision quest occurred when the quester traveled alone into the wilderness. During this time, he had no food, water, or sleep. He was supposed to focus his mind, heart, and body on nature and what it means to be human. At some point, usually after a few days, the quester would receive a vision. It was like a dream, but the quester was not asleep. This vision carried powerful meaning. Some people claimed to have conversations with the spirits or their ancestors. Others claimed to be able to see into the future. After his time in the wilderness, the quester returned and shared his vision with the tribe's holy man or woman, who helped him understand exactly what it meant. This vision would help to guide his actions and decisions for the rest of his life.

The quester traveled alone into the wilderness.

The Importance of the Buffalo

For the Lakota and other tribes of the Great Plains, there was no greater symbol of the connection between people and nature than the buffalo. Some tribes on the Plains grew crops, especially corn, and they gathered various wild plants, but buffalo were always the main source of food. These are the largest animals in North America, heavier than even the biggest moose or grizzly bear. At one time, massive buffalo herds ruled the Great Plains. There were millions of them, and the earth trembled beneath their thundering hooves.

North American buffalo (bison)

Buffalo were valued for far more than their meat. In fact, Plains tribes used every part of the animal: blood, bones, hide, intestines, and organs; everything had a purpose. After a kill, the best meat was eaten right away, and the rest of it was dried and stored for later use. Hides were used for such things as clothing, tipi covers, bedding, and moccasins. The hair was used to make rope, pillows, or ornaments. The bones were used to make hand tools or ceremonial costumes, and some were used to make toys for children. Buffalo horns became cups, ladles, or ornaments for headdresses. The stomach and intestines were made into pouches and buckets. Blood was used as paint or as the base for a tasty bowl of soup. Sinew, the tough tissue connecting muscle to bone, was used for thread, bowstrings, and glue.

Another important buffalo product was something people could find on the ground anywhere the buffalo had passed: the dung or droppings, also known as buffalo chips. Dried buffalo chips were the main source of fuel for campfires. (They did not smell bad because they were little more than digested clumps of grass, which was the only thing the buffalo ever ate.) There were some trees on the Plains, and people could find firewood if they needed it. But Plains tribes did not have access to large forests like tribes in the Great Basin or Northwest Plateau. Plains tribes used some wood to make the frames for their tipis and sleds, or litters, to haul their belongings from one camp to another. Otherwise, almost everything they needed in order to survive came from the buffalo.

Home Sweet Home

Most tribes of the Plains and neighboring regions were seminomadic. This means that they did not live in one place all year long. For example, Plains tribes usually followed the buffalo, but they also went to special camps during the frigid winters. Tipis were built using only buffalo hides and wooden poles, but they could stand up to thunderstorms and blizzards.

Tribes of the Great Basin built domed houses called wigwams, or wickiups, which were cozy and safe in all kinds of weather. A wigwam had a frame made of flexible sticks over which were placed sheets of bark or mats woven from grass and leaves. Like tipis, wigwams were portable, which was important because Great Basin tribes also moved from place to place in search of food. They did not have buffalo. Instead, they gathered nuts and berries, and they hunted for smaller game like rabbits and deer. They had access to good clay, so they made pottery. They used stone tools. Stones could be reshaped and sharpened for use as heads for arrows, spears, and axes, as well as made into tools for digging, scraping, grinding, and other daily tasks.

Wigwams were cozy and warm.

People of the Plateau lived in wigwam-type lodges, too. There, the soil was dry, and food was sometimes hard to find. There were few edible plants, and it was hard to grow crops. Hunters were lucky if they were able to find a jackrabbit, deer, or occasional bear. However, the Plateau tribes did not need to search for food on land; all the nearby rivers and streams were loaded with big, tasty salmon and other fish! The Plateau tribes were as good at fishing as the Plains tribes were at hunting buffalo.

The Mandan

Not all tribes of the Plains and surrounding regions were nomadic. Some, like the Mandan, learned to grow corn, beans, and other crops. They hunted for buffalo, too, but they grew enough food so that they did not need to move and follow the herd. They could afford to build permanent villages and wait for the buffalo to come to them. During their westward adventure, explorers Lewis and Clark encountered the Mandan and wrote about their way of life. They were impressed with the size and wealth of the villages. There may have been over 15,000 Mandan living in nine large villages. In addition to farming and hunting, they were active traders. They traded various animal furs, buffalo products, and crops with surrounding tribes. Later, after more contact with traders and settlers from the United States, the Mandan traded guns and horses.

Mandan village

Devastating Changes

Back in the early 1800s, when Lewis and Clark passed through on their famous expedition to find out what was on the other side of the Mississippi, no one could have guessed just how much and how quickly life would change for all the tribes of the Plains, Basin, and Plateau. The introduction of horses had already changed the way Native Americans traveled, hunted, and fought. Guns also made a big difference in their lives. But horses and guns were not the only things the Europeans brought. They brought diseases, too. Disease took a very heavy **toll** on the Mandan because they lived closely together in such large villages and rarely moved around. In one Mandan village in 1837, smallpox infected and killed all but 125 out of 1,600 people.

The Plains buffalo were also greatly affected by the arrival of Europeans. Buffalo hides made into leather were valuable to people in the cities on the East Coast. With their guns, hunters could kill as many buffalo as they wanted. How many did they kill? Consider this: in 1804, there were as many as 60 million buffalo roaming the Plains; in 1890, there were fewer than 1,000.

By 1890, the buffalo and many of the native people were no longer living in the Great Plains. Many of the tribes were forced to leave their homelands and make way for settlers, railroads, and cities of the United States. Native American culture, language, and customs survived, but their way of life was seriously damaged.

Herd of North American buffalo (bison)

Chapter 3

Tales from the Great Plains

THE BIG QUESTION
What do these Native American stories reveal about the culture of the Comanche and the Lakota Sioux?

The image of a brave warrior on horseback gazing over his beloved prairie or canyon is perhaps one of the things that comes to mind when we think of Native Americans. Horses were, and remain, essential to many Native American cultures. But there was a time, long ago, when Native Americans did not know about horses.

When Native Americans first saw the Spanish conquistadors on their horses, they wondered if man and horse were one beast, for they had never seen a human riding any kind of animal. The Comanche soon realized this was not true, but many years would pass before they learned to talk to the horses and ride them like the Spaniards.

There was once a great horse that all the Comanche feared. This horse ran wild on the prairies, and none of the Comanche would go near him, for he was fierce and powerful. They let him roam and never tried to catch him. The horse was easy to identify because he always wore a saddle and the **remnants** of a blue, silk blanket on his back. This is a story of how the horse with the blue blanket came to roam free on the prairie.

The Swift Blue One (Comanche)

One day, a brave young Comanche warrior was out hunting when he saw a Spanish soldier riding on a horse. The soldier wore heavy metal armor, and he carried a gun and a long, sharp sword. Perhaps this soldier was lost, or perhaps he was a ***scout*** *sent to discover what was over the next hill. The young Comanche warrior and his people considered the Spanish to be enemies, for the Spanish, with their guns, sharp steel swords, and powerful horses, sometimes attacked the Comanche camps.*

Fear and anger rushed through the Comanche's veins, and he rose from his hiding place in the tall grass and shot an arrow at the Spaniard. The arrow found its way through a crack in the soldier's armor, and he fell from his horse to the ground with a loud thud. Wounded, he moaned in pain. His horse stood over him and did not move.

The Comanche wanted to approach the Spaniard to inspect his strange weapons and armor, but when he drew near, the horse snorted angrily and beat his front hooves on the ground. The Comanche was afraid of the horse and he backed away. He wanted the horse to leave, so he snarled and growled and yelled at him, but the horse still did not budge. The Comanche did not speak the horse language, and he did not know what to do next.

The Spaniard could see that the Comanche wanted to talk to the horse. Using sign language, the Spaniard told the Comanche that he would teach him the horse language if the Comanche would spare his life. The Comanche agreed. The Spaniard taught the Comanche the words people use to make the horse go and stop, walk and gallop. The Comanche repeated the words again and again until he knew them and could say them to the horse.

The Comanche tried to save the Spaniard's life, but the arrow was too deep, and he died anyway. The horse had a soft blue blanket and a saddle on its back. The Comanche did not remove either because he thought the horse wanted them. Then the Comanche got onto the horse's back and spoke the horse language, and the horse carried him back to camp.

The other Comanche were amazed when they saw him. He told them his story and showed them how he had learned to make the horse go and stop, walk and gallop. After that, the Comanche warrior always rode the horse, and he became a fearsome warrior and a great hunter. He named the horse The Swift Blue One because he was as fast as the wind. The other warriors were afraid of the horse, and they thought he would ride over them and crush them with his big hooves.

One day, the warrior was killed in battle, but The Swift Blue One survived. The other Comanche were still afraid of the horse, so they set him free to roam on the prairie. They would see him out there sometimes, running as fast as the wind, with a saddle and blue blanket on his back.

In time, more horses escaped from the Spanish soldiers, and these horses joined The Swift Blue One out on the prairie. He became their chief, and they followed him everywhere. The Swift Blue One's herd grew and grew, until there were too many horses to count. Eventually, other Comanche learned the horse language, and the horse culture spread. Many of the horses ridden by the Sioux, Apache, Pawnee, and other tribes of the Great Plains and beyond are the descendants of The Swift Blue One.

White Buffalo Calf Woman (Lakota Sioux)

On the Great Plains, among the Lakota and other Sioux nations, it was customary for young people to embark on a Vision Quest. A Vision Quest helped to guide a young person's actions and decisions as an adult. The Vision Quest was just one of seven sacred ceremonies practiced by the Lakota. According to Lakota legend, the people learned these seven ceremonies from White Buffalo Calf Woman.

Many years ago, when the Sioux people were young and had not learned their way in the world, the ***bands*** *of the Lakota tribe met for a* ***council****. This was during a terribly hot summer when the land was parched and the buffalo had moved so far away that the people could not find them. This was before the Sioux had horses, so they had to travel on foot and sometimes they could not keep up with the buffalo.*

Two brave young men went out to scout for buffalo. They searched everywhere, but they could find no signs of buffalo or anything else to eat. One day, they saw a hill and decided to climb up to see what they could see. In the distance, they spied something strange coming toward them. At first they could only make out a small speck, and they could not tell whether it was moving on the ground or in the air.

As it neared, they saw that it was a human figure. As it came nearer still, they could see that it was a beautiful young woman. She wore clothing of bright, white, buckskin decorated with beautiful, colorful designs. Two dark braids of hair dangled down, and she had red dots painted on each cheek. The two men could see that she was no ordinary woman. They realized she was a ***wakan****, a sacred and powerful thing.*

One of the men trembled with fear as the wakan stranger approached. The other, however, was smitten with love. "She is the most beautiful woman I have ever seen," he told his friend. "I want to marry her."

"Do not go near her," said the other. "You must respect her and do as she says."

But the love-struck man did not listen to these wise words. Instead, he approached the wakan stranger. Suddenly, a cloud of smoke enveloped both

One of the men trembled with fear as the wakan stranger approached. The other, however, was smitten with love.

of them. The other man could not see through the smoke, but when it finally cleared, the woman was alone, and all that remained of his friend was a pile of scorched bones!

Truly afraid, the young man raised his bow and pointed an arrow at her. But she said, "Do not harm me. I am White Buffalo Calf Woman, and I bring good things for you and your people."

The young man dropped his bow and listened, comforted by her kind words.

"Go home and tell your chief to raise the medicine tepee and prepare for my arrival. In four days I will bring my gifts to your people."

So the young man hurried home and shared the news. Some people did not believe him. They thought he must be crazy with hunger. But the chief heard the words and commanded his people to raise the great medicine tepee, the largest tepee, which they used for the holiest ceremonies.

Sure enough, four days later the people saw the White Buffalo Calf Woman approaching the camp. In her arms she carried a large bundle.

The chief invited her into the medicine tepee. Inside, she told the people to make an altar of red earth in the middle of the tepee and to place a buffalo skull upon it. She also told them to make a small rack using three sticks. Then she opened her bundle and removed a special object, the sacred pipe, called chanunpa, *which she placed on the rack.*

Into the pipe she put bark of the red willow tree, and she placed a buffalo chip on the fire. The buffalo chip made the everlasting fire, the fire to be passed from generation to generation. Then she lit the pipe. "The smoke of this pipe is the breath of the Great Spirit, Tunkashila," she said. She taught the people to pray using the sacred pipe. "With your feet on the ground and the smoke of the pipe rising to the sky, this pipe forms the connection between you and the Great Spirit."

She taught them the pipe-filling song, and how to raise the pipe toward Grandfather Sky, and then toward Grandmother Earth, and then in all four directions. She continued, "The wooden stem of the pipe represents all the things that grow on the earth. The bowl at the end of the stem is the buffalo, which is the flesh and blood of your people. Twelve feathers hanging from the stem represent the spotted eagle, messenger of the Great Spirit. And engraved in the bowl there are seven circles. These are the seven sacred ceremonies you will practice with the pipe."

These are the seven ceremonies she taught the people: the Sacred Pipe Ceremony; the Sweat Lodge; the Vision Quest; the Sun Dance; the Making of Relatives; the Keeping of the Soul; and the Preparing of a Girl for Womanhood. These are the seven ceremonies practiced by the Lakota Sioux, which they learned from White Buffalo Calf Woman.

Chapter 4

The Changing Landscape of California

THE BIG QUESTION
What impact did the arrival of explorers, miners, missionaries, and settlers in what is now California have on Native Americans' way of life?

At the eastern edge of California's Central Valley, where the grassland meets the jagged Sierra Nevada Mountains, there is a city named Oroville. In Spanish, *oro* is the word for gold. This city was once a small town. The town earned its name during the California Gold Rush, when thousands of gold prospectors flocked to the valley in search of quick riches. Oroville was just one of many lawless, rowdy towns that sprang up all over northern California during that time.

Most people who joined the Gold Rush never did find much gold. However, they did find other forms of wealth. Oroville was at the head of the Feather River, just beneath the Sierra Nevada Mountains. Supplies for the gold miners were shipped up that river from Sacramento. People who lived in Oroville did not need to look for gold, because they grew rich selling shovels and food to the miners up in the hills.

When the Gold Rush ended, pioneers moved in and carved up the land into farms. Thanks to warm, sunny summers, wet winters, and rich soil, the Central Valley was perfect for farming. A few years later, the Transcontinental Railroad was finished, linking California to the rest of the United States. The railroad passed right through downtown Oroville, making it possible for Central Valley farmers to send their goods to markets all over the country.

Oroville Dam is on the Feather River, east of the city of Oroville. It is the tallest dam in the U.S. Next to the dam is Lake Oroville. Lake Oroville is the second largest man-made lake in California. Long before there was a dam, or a reservoir, Native Americans lived on this land.

Ishi, Lone Survivor

It was in downtown Oroville, in the summer of 1911, many years after the Gold Rush of the 1840s and 1850s, that a middle-aged man named Ishi, the last of his people, emerged from the wilderness. It was a hot, dry summer, just like every summer in the Valley. A few nights before, a thunderstorm had rolled through, and a bolt of lightning had started a wildfire in the dry, grassy foothills across the river. Oroville was safe from the flames, but the winds blew smoke through the town for many days. Ishi must have looked like a ghost to anyone who saw him sneaking down the smoke-filled street. He wore only a tattered **loincloth** made of rabbit hide, and he carried a bow and small **quiver** of arrows. Ishi was starving, alone, and scared.

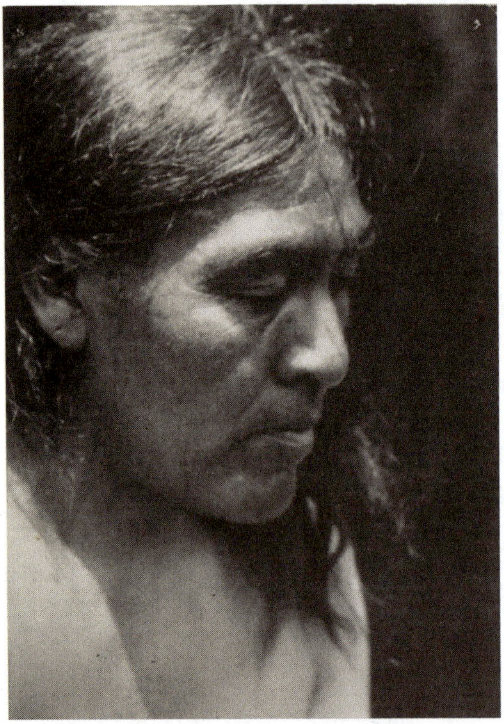

Ishi in the summer of 1911

There was a time when settlers lived alongside Native Americans in California's Central Valley. Indeed, there was a time when Native Americans were the *only* people living in what is now California. But in 1911, Ishi was a very unusual sight. He was certainly not the last Native American in California, but he was probably the last to leave the woods and the old way of living. He was certainly the last of his tribe, the Yahi people.

Why do we still remember a lonely, hungry man named Ishi, who was searching for food on that smoky, hot summer day? What had happened to the rest of his people and all the other native tribes of California? Unfortunately, the story of what happened to the Native American population of California presents a sad, dark chapter in American history. The Native Americans of California were pushed aside to make way for gold mines, railroads, farms, towns, and cities.

It is impossible to know exact numbers, but best estimates are that there were around 300,000 Native Americans in California when the first Spanish settlers arrived. There were well over 100 different tribes and a wide variety of cultures, languages, and customs. Mostly, they lived in small villages ranging from a hundred to a thousand people. There were no formal borders or property lines, but each tribe was adapted to life in a specific area.

All the California tribes lived a hunter-gatherer lifestyle. Acorns were a major source of food throughout the region. Acorns are nuts from the oak tree. You would not want to eat an acorn raw because the taste is very bitter. But if you grind it up into flour and soak it, you can remove most of the bitterness and use it to make tasty bread. Fish were another major food source for many tribes. The tribes caught fish from the ocean, the rivers, and the lakes. Besides acorns and fish, each region had various animals and plants for people to hunt and gather, such as rabbits and deer, plus various roots, berries, and other gifts from nature.

Trade was also an important part of tribal life in California. If they could not find what they needed in nature, the people could trade with a neighboring tribe. Coastal tribes had access to lots of fish, but they needed more acorns. Inland tribes had plenty of acorns but not always enough meat. Tribes in the central mountains had access to a special rock called obsidian, or volcanic glass, which was valuable for making razor-sharp arrowheads and knives. Obsidian was far more valuable to Native Americans than gold or silver. They did not find too much use for those metals, though they did know where to find them.

Canoes played an essential role in the culture and lifestyle of nearly every California tribe. Different regions made different kinds of canoes. In southern California, they built big *tomols* out of wooden planks. Only specially trained craftsmen could build them, and they never shared their secrets! *Tomols* could carry several paddlers and hundreds of pounds of trade goods. Best of all, the sturdy, speedy *tomols* were seaworthy, so southern tribes could paddle up the coast and trade with northern tribes.

Tomols carried several paddlers.

In the Central Valley, the people made their canoes by weaving long, tough reeds, or river grass. There they did not need to paddle into the rough ocean. Instead, they had wide, lazy rivers and sparkling lakes. And all the way up north, where the great redwood trees grow up into the clouds, people made dugout canoes from hollowed-out logs. Dugout canoes were tough enough for the ocean but also **nimble** enough to survive the wild mountain rivers.

Daily life focused on securing enough food for everyone. Fortunately, California was a land of plenty, so if everyone worked hard there was usually enough food to go around. In good years, there was more than enough food, so the people had time for other things. Basket-weaving was common throughout California. Tribes of the Central Valley were highly skilled, producing a variety of colorful baskets in all shapes and sizes.

Weaving was an important skill.

There was also time for fun and games. In northern California, children enjoyed a game similar to soccer. The boys and girls all played together. Boys were only allowed to kick the ball, whereas the girls could kick it, throw it, or carry it into the goal. However, a boy was also allowed to pick up a girl and carry her into the goal with the ball!

Ball game not unlike soccer

A *tule* was a round, one-room hut.

As with all Native Americans, the people of California built their houses using the best materials available in their home territory. Southern tribes used small trees and reeds to build *tules.* A *tule* was a round, one-room hut. Despite being made from reeds, *tules* were strong, able to withstand wind and rain, and cozy enough for mild, southern California winters. The Miwok people and other tribes of central and northern California preferred the *umacha,* which was shaped like a tipi but made of long wooden rails instead of buffalo hide. Farther north, in the redwood forests, the Wiyot people and their northern neighbors built stout, sturdy houses out of redwood planks.

Roundhouses were the central feature in most villages. No matter what type of houses they built, and no matter whether the tribe was large or small, wealthy or poor, there was almost always a roundhouse in the middle of the village. The roundhouse was used for ceremonies and important meetings. The roundhouse was also where the tribal religious leaders, or *shamans,* carried out important rituals.

Religious beliefs reflected a close connection to the cycles of nature and to animals. While all tribes had unique beliefs, myths, and rituals, the people generally believed they shared a special kinship or bond with other living things. They felt fortunate and thankful to live in a place with so many resources.

Tules could withstand wind and rain.

The Wiyot tribe of the north, with their dugout canoes and stout wooden homes, held the World Renewal Ceremony each autumn. This special dance marked the beginning of a new year. The World Renewal Ceremony was hosted by the wealthiest village. Everyone was invited, and nobody was ever turned away. The dance could go on for seven days or more. Although there

Wiyot World Renewal Ceremony

was feasting and great fun, the ceremony had a serious purpose. The people showed their respect for nature and prayed for a good year ahead. California was a land of plenty, but there were always challenges and dangers. The Wiyot hoped their ceremony would help prevent natural disasters such as earthquakes, floods, or failure of the acorn crop.

Spanish settlers colonized California beginning in the mid-1700s and things changed quickly for Native Americans. Instead of trying to push the California tribes out of the way, the Spanish sent missionaries to persuade the people to change their way of life. Missionaries were determined to convert the native people to Christianity, to educate and, in their minds, "civilize" them, and to teach them to become farmers. A typical mission included a church and new houses for Native Americans, plus thousands of acres of farmland.

However, while the missionaries offered peace, they had brought soldiers with them, too. They gave the tribes a choice: live at the mission, or fight against these soldiers. Once they moved to the missions, Native Americans had to dress like Europeans. They had to stop practicing their own beliefs and customs. Mostly, however, they worked the farmland—essentially a kind of forced labor.

Not surprisingly, many tribes did not want to give up their homelands. At first, the Spanish could not force many people to move. However, without even realizing it, European explorers and settlers brought a deadly weapon to the Americas: disease. Smallpox and other illnesses devastated Native American populations in southern California. The people had no **immunity** to these diseases. Within a few years, some tribes were almost totally wiped out. The survivors had little choice but to live at the missions.

Eventually, the Native American groups of northern California suffered a similar fate. First came the explorers, followed by the miners and the settlers. These new arrivals were all hungry for the land and its resources. They came by the thousands to mine and to build farms and railroads and cities. They had guns, plus help from the U.S. Army, and they were determined to own every inch of valuable land in California. Tribes were forced to move onto small reservation lands. Those who refused were often massacred.

Remember Ishi, the "wild" man who emerged from the wilderness in Oroville? When he was just a boy, his people, the Yahi, refused to move off their land. Gold miners attacked Ishi's village and killed most of his family and friends. He and a handful of others managed to survive in the wild. Years passed, and one by one, all the other Yahi died. At last, only Ishi remained in the woods and canyons where his ancestors once lived. Hungry and tired, with no place left to go, Ishi finally came in from the wilderness.

Ishi did find a place in modern society. He devoted much of the rest of his life to teaching anthropologists about the Yahi language, mythology, and customs. The Yahi tribe is gone now, but in some ways the culture lives on, and Ishi's knowledge remains for everyone to learn.

It is also important to note that, today, there are still over 100 tribes in California. They do not all live according to all the old traditions and lifestyles, but there has been a major revival of traditional Native American culture and tribal life over the past several decades. In fact, there are twice as many Native Americans in California today as there were when the first Spanish explorers arrived. Some live on reservations, and some still practice the ancient arts and customs. In the north, the Wiyot still hold World Renewal Ceremonies each year. Despite terrible hardships endured by their ancestors, these proud people continue to ensure that their culture survives.

Native Americans continue to celebrate their culture.

Chapter 5

Rainforests, Rivers, and Ocean

THE BIG QUESTION
Prior to the arrival of Europeans, how did the habitat of the Pacific Northwest influence the culture of local Native American tribes?

What do you imagine when you think of a rainforest? Perhaps you imagine a hot, humid place with heavy vegetation and trees filled with exotic parrots and monkeys. You might also imagine snakes and all sorts of bugs. It is true that most rainforests are steamy jungles located in tropical regions of the Americas, Africa, and Asia. However, not all rainforests are in the tropics. Some rainforests grow in the temperate zone, where the weather is never too hot or too cold, but it is often very wet.

The Pacific Northwest region includes much of Washington State and Oregon, plus the western flank of Canada, called British Columbia. Temperate rainforest blankets the coastal parts of this region. The steady rains and mild temperatures are perfect for plant growth. Spruce, hemlock, and fir trees can reach heights of 300 feet or more. Beneath the dense treetop canopy, the forest floor is a carpet of thick mosses, fluffy ferns, and lichens. The climate is good for animal life, too. There are hundreds of different bird and fish species. There are at least 140 different mammals, including some very large elk, bighorn sheep, mountain lions, gray wolves, and the occasional grizzly bear.

Fishing for Salmon

The Pacific Northwest is also a good habitat for humans. By some estimates, Native Americans have lived there for as many as 500 generations, or 15,000 years. The area was once home to at least 30 tribes, hundreds of villages, and a huge variety of languages, customs, and beliefs. All the tribes had a hunter-gatherer lifestyle, but they did not need to move around in order to find food. They lived in large, permanent villages. They did not need to farm either. Everything they needed was readily available in the forests and waters. As long as they respected those resources, then there was always enough to go around. In fact, there was usually more than enough for everyone.

A very important food source for most tribes was salmon. They could always depend on salmon to swim up the rivers every year. One important thing to know about salmon is that they are born in rivers, but they live most of their lives at sea. When they are adults, they return from the sea and swim back up the rivers, to the very same places where they were born. There, they lay their eggs and die. The eggs hatch, the baby salmon find their way to the sea, and the cycle continues.

The other important thing to know about salmon is that they are very nutritious! The people of the Pacific Northwest certainly knew this, and they became master fishermen. Some tribes fished using baskets, nets, spears or **harpoons**, and a variety of ingenious traps to catch salmon.

However, salmon are only available to catch in the rivers for a few months each year, when they return to lay their eggs. For the remainder of the year, they are in the ocean. Therefore, if you depend on salmon for food, you will have to **supplement** your diet. Native American men in this region hunted the big mammals that roamed the rainforests. Women gathered roots, berries, and grains, including wild rice. Many tribes went after other types of fish, as well as whales and seals, the mammals of the sea.

The Whale Hunters

One tribe, the Makah, were famous whalers. They used long, fast canoes to chase whales in the rough Pacific waters, and they killed them with long, sharp harpoons. This is how they hunted huge gray whales and humpbacks, which can weigh up to 80,000 pounds (about the same as four school buses). Imagine hunting a creature that size from the front of a canoe with a harpoon! This was very dangerous work, but it was worth the risk, because one whale could feed a whole village for months. After they killed a whale, the hunters towed it to shore and the whole village would come out to help cut up the meat, salt it, and hang it up to dry.

This preserved the meat for later use. Just as Plains tribes used all parts of the buffalo, Pacific Coast tribes used the whole whale. They took oil from the whale's blubber to use for cooking, **tanning** hides, or covering wounds and bug bites. Whale oil was also valuable in trade to inland tribes. Bones were used to make scrapers, fishhooks, and other tools.

The Makah were, and still are, expert whalers.

The Power of the Totem

Like other Native Americans, the people of the Pacific Northwest did not take anything for granted. After they hunted any animal—whether it was a salmon, whale, elk, or anything else—they always welcomed its spirit into their village and thanked it for helping them. People felt a direct connection to other living things, and they expressed this connection through their religion.

Tribes of the Pacific Northwest practiced a form of religion called *totemism*. They believed that people shared special bonds with animals, as though their spirits were connected. Every family had a bond with a specific animal spirit. This animal was the family's *totem*. In many tribes, totems were displayed on colorful, artistic woodcarvings. Some people placed a tall *totem pole* outside the family home. Others passed a sacred mask down from generation to generation.

The totems were not simply for decoration. They were symbols of something far more significant than a fancy woodcarving. A totem was the key to a family's **identity**. Just as every animal has its own unique traits, so too did a totem have unique meaning for the family. Some totems were big, fierce animals, like the bear, wolf, or eagle. Others were gentler animals, like the beaver or seal. The size or strength of the animal was not as important as the stories and characteristics of the animal. For instance, beavers were symbols of determination, wolves were symbols of loyalty, whales represented wisdom, and spiders represented creativity.

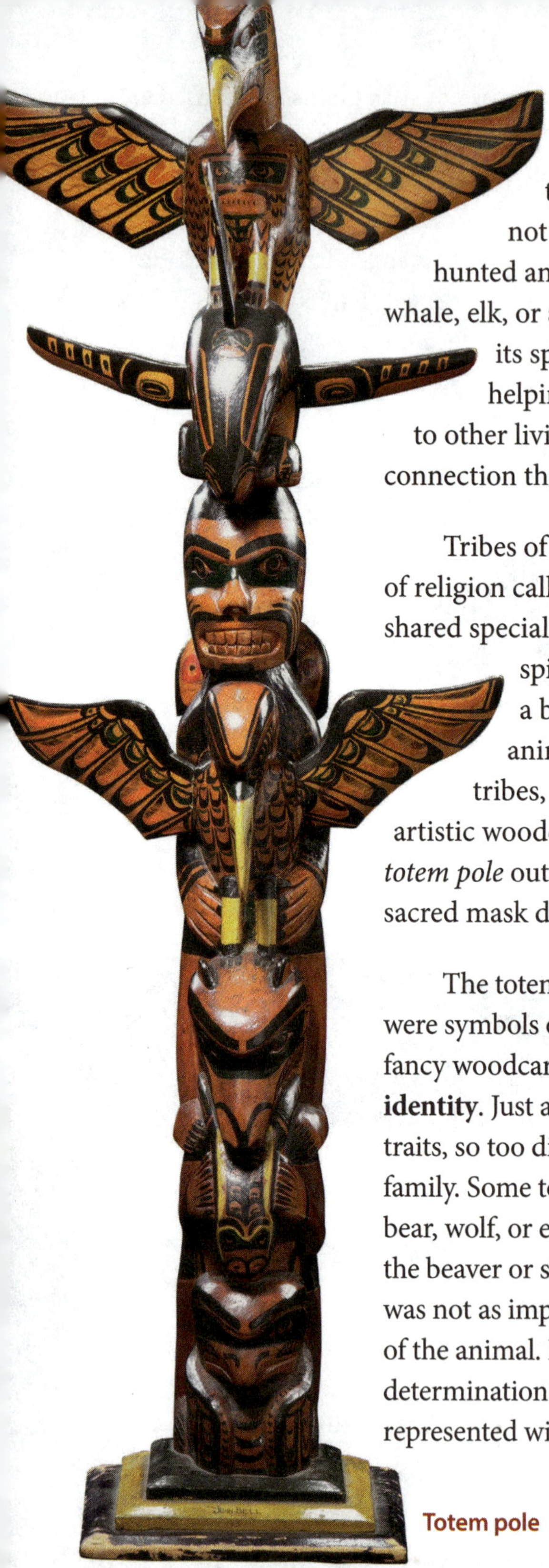

Totem pole

In some tribes, a family could not hunt, eat, or otherwise harm its totem animal. Not all totems were animals, though. Some family totems were related to other parts of nature, like the rivers, the wind, or the sun and moon. Some totems included mythical creatures and monsters, like the powerful Thunderbird or the two-headed Sea Serpent. Each symbol and the stories related to it were passed from generation to generation, so they carried special meaning for the family.

Clans and the Potlatch

The social structure of Pacific Northwest tribes was centered around large, extended families called clans. Clans lived in spacious homes called plank houses: long, narrow buildings made of cedar planks. As many as 50 or more people could live in one plank house.

A single tribe or village had many clans, and although they all worked together and shared their resources, some clans were much wealthier than others. The head of a clan was a chieftain, and the wealthiest chieftains were very powerful. Most importantly, they had the power to decide who was allowed to hunt, fish, or gather foods in certain places.

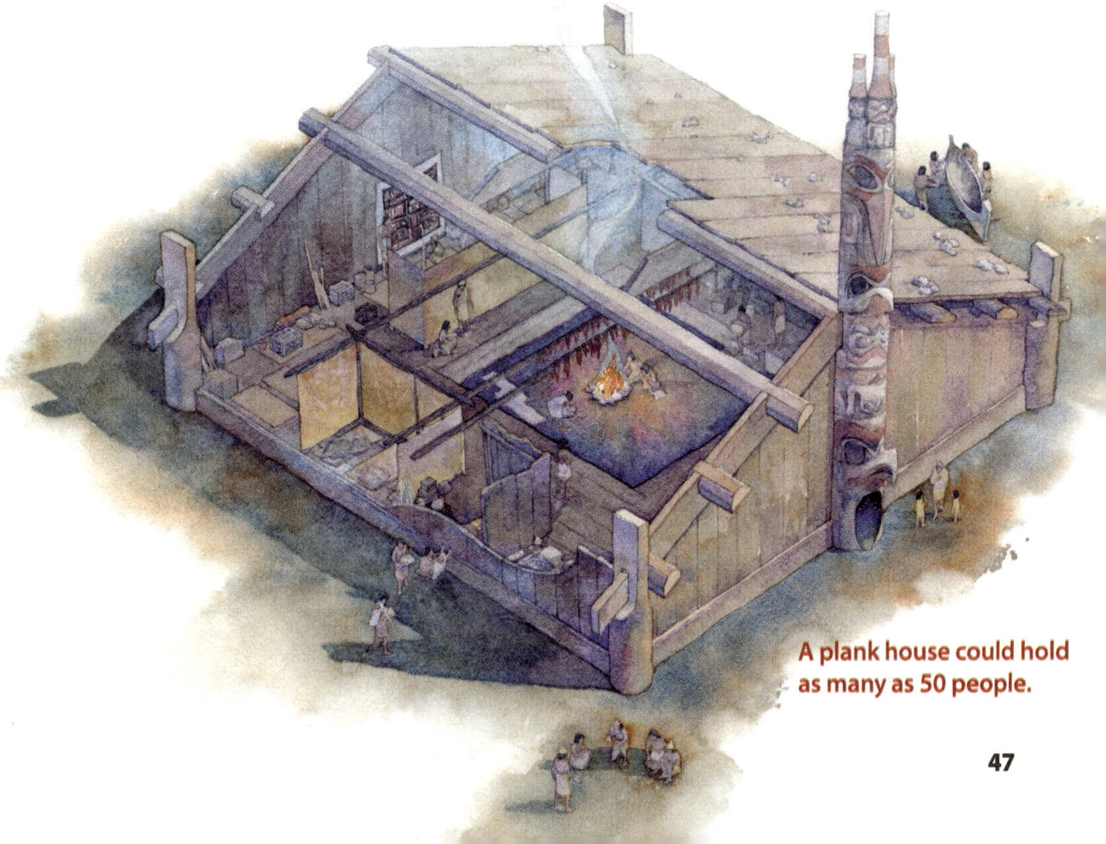

A plank house could hold as many as 50 people.

Perhaps the most **distinct** and interesting tradition among tribes of the Pacific Northwest was the *potlatch* ceremony. A potlatch was basically a huge party. Every tribe had different rituals and rules about how to celebrate a potlatch, but they all had the same basic purpose: to display someone's wealth. Only the richest chieftains hosted potlatches, often to celebrate or mark a birth, death, marriage, or other important event within the clan. Wealthy chieftains had special plank houses specially built just for potlatches. The richer the host, the bigger the potlatch. Sometimes, they invited the whole village, along with chieftains from wealthy clans in other villages.

A potlatch could last for days or even several weeks, depending on the host's wealth and tribal customs. There were lavish feasts, storytelling and speeches, and lots of singing and dancing. Potlatches also involved important, secretive religious rituals. However, gift-giving was always the main feature. In fact, the word *potlatch* means "giving," and this is the unique thing that separates potlatches from other Native American ceremonies.

A potlach could last for days.

The potlatch host did not give gifts just because he was kind and generous. The gifts were a display or expression of his power and wealth. Gifts included blankets, animal hides, and shiny copper ornaments. Ordinarily, the hosts did not give food as gifts, although they did supply food for the feasts.

Hide

Wealth among the people of the Pacific Northwest was not measured by how much someone owned but by how much they gave away to others. Chieftains also used potlatches to award ranks, or seats, to their friends and family members. This is how people in the tribe moved up the social ladder. The closer a person's seat was to the chieftain, the more power and privilege that person had within the clan.

Blankets

Copper bracelets

Sometimes gifts were burned.

In some tribes, they not only gave away their wealth, they also destroyed it. They built great bonfires and burned the gifts, to show that they were so wealthy they did not need any of it. Potlatches created competition among the various chieftains. If a chieftain went to a potlatch and received gifts from another chieftain, then he was expected to host a potlatch and give even *more* gifts. If one chieftain burned a big pile of blankets and animal hides at his potlatch, then the other chieftains would hold potlatches and burn even more blankets and hides. In this way, the amount of gift-giving always increased, as each chieftain tried to make his potlatch bigger than the last.

European Contact

With European contact, tribes of the Pacific Northwest suffered many of the same problems as tribes in other regions. Disease and warfare spread quickly, and by the mid-1800s, the populations were greatly reduced. Tribes lost access to their traditional fishing and hunting grounds as miners, loggers, and other settlers moved into the region. One after another, the tribes were forced onto small reservations, or their numbers dwindled.

For many years, potlatches were outlawed by the U.S. government. They did not understand why Native Americans destroyed such valuable resources. Sometimes the potlatch hosts even melted and destroyed copper coins they earned through trade with the settlers. This seemed very foolish and wasteful to outsiders. In many cases, Native Americans were also forbidden from displaying their sacred totems because settlers believed these were connected to some kind of witchcraft. To the tribes of the Pacific Northwest, the potlatches and totems were the heart of their culture and identity. Without them, the people lost their connection to the past, and they struggled to understand their own purpose or place in the world.

Despite this, many tribes in the Pacific Northwest held on to their traditions. They still pass totems from one generation to the next. They still share their ancient myths and stories about ancestors and animal spirits. And, in some places, they still host potlatches to celebrate the great events in life and all the gifts of nature.

Modern potlatch ceremony

Chapter 6

Myths from the Pacific Northwest

THE BIG QUESTION
How did tribes of the Pacific Northwest use myths to explain things in nature?

Raven Steals the Light

Raven is a very important character in the mythology of most Pacific Northwest tribes. He is featured in numerous stories, many of which are creation myths. Creation myths explain how the world began and how people and various animals came into the world. However, in this tale, Raven is not really a creator. He is actually a trickster, meaning that he makes things happen by tricking other characters. The following story explains how light was hidden and then restored.

Many years ago, in a house on the banks of the Yakima River, there lived an old man and his grown daughter. You would not have known by looking at his little house, but the old man was very rich. However, he was also very greedy. Every year, many salmon swam past his house. He always caught many more than he needed, and he chased away anyone else who tried to catch them. "Go away!" he yelled. "Those are my fish."

"These are not your fish," the people told him. "The river gave them to us."

But the old man ignored them. "You'll be sorry if you take my fish again," he warned.

When he saw a woman gathering firewood in the forest near his house, the old man yelled, "That is my firewood! Go away and find your own."

The woman held up the sticks and said, "You do not own this wood. The tree gave it to me."

The old man only shook his fists and warned, "You'll be sorry if you take my firewood again!"

The old man was so greedy that he would not even share with his own daughter. He would not let her take fish from the river. She was allowed to gather roots and berries to eat, but only if she walked far away from the house so she would not gather any of his foods. When he caught her eating blackberries from a bush near the house, he yelled, "Those are my berries! You'll be sorry you took them!"

"But the bush gave them to me," his daughter said, in a ***meek****, nervous voice.*

This made the old man very angry. He was tired of people stealing from him, but he knew how to stop them once and for all. People could not steal his things if they could not see them. However, he was so rich, he could not hide all the things he owned, so he decided to hide the light instead.

The old man took the sun and moon and all the stars from the sky, and he put them in a box. He hid the box in his house and refused to tell anyone where it was. Then the whole world was dark. When people needed firewood, they had to crawl out into the darkness and search the ground with their hands until they found something that felt like wood. When they were hungry, they had to crawl into the river and feel around in the water until a fish swam into their hands.

Life without light was very hard, and soon the people were cold and hungry, and a sadness filled their hearts. But Raven heard about the greedy old man who stole the sun and moon and stars, and he came up with a plan to steal them back!

Raven followed the old man's daughter when she went out searching for food. She searched in the darkness and found a blackberry bush. The thorns pricked her fingers as she searched for berries. Clever Raven turned himself into a blackberry, and she picked him and ate him. Then Raven was in her belly, and he became her child.

Months later, Raven was born. The old man did not like having a baby in the house. To make matters worse, Raven grew very quickly, and soon he was a curious, energetic boy. He asked questions about everything, and he always wanted the old man to tell him stories, sing songs, and play games. The old man did not like to do any of these things, but Raven asked him every day, anyway.

"Grandfather, I am bored," Raven said. "Will you play a game with me?"

"No."

"Will you tell me a story?"

"No."

"Then what can I do? I am bored!"

The old man fumbled around in the dark, trying to find something for Raven to play with. Raven refused everything he offered. "I already played with that. That is boring," Raven said. "If only I could see, then maybe I could find something to do. But it is too dark."

Then the old man had an idea. He went to his secret hiding place and pulled out the box. He gave the box to Raven and said, "Here, play with this. This will keep you busy for a while. Just don't show anybody else! Now, leave me alone."

Raven opened the box, and the light of the sun and moon shone on his face. Then the old man could see that he had been tricked! Grasping the box in his talons, Raven flapped his wings and flew out of the house. He flew and flew, way up high into the sky, and there he emptied the box, and the sun and moon and stars all returned to their places, and the light was restored.

Thunderbird and Killer Whale

Thunderbird is a mythical creature common in most Pacific Northwest cultures. It is also a common theme on totem poles or ceremonial costumes. In most stories, Thunderbird was a kind and powerful creature who often helped people. The story of Thunderbird and Killer Whale appears in many tribal mythologies. Like many myths, this one was used to explain certain aspects of nature or important events. There are two natural events, or phenomena, explained in this story. Can you tell what they are?

One day Killer Whale arrived in the waters and attacked all the other fish. Killer Whale was hungry, and he ate many fish. The fish he did not eat were so scared they swam away to other waters. Then, the people could not find any fish for themselves and they began to starve.

Thunderbird was a big, mighty bird. His bright, colorful feathers were as long as canoe paddles, and his talons were like harpoons. When he flapped his great wings, the sound of thunder rumbled through the skies.

One day, Thunderbird was flying along the coast. He looked down and saw that the people were starving. This made Thunderbird sad, because he loved the people and did not want to see them suffer. He asked them why they did not have any fish, and the people told him about Killer Whale. This made Thunderbird very angry.

Thunderbird found Killer Whale and swooped down out of the sky. Thunderbird grabbed Killer Whale with his talons and tried to carry him away, but Killer Whale put up a fight. He wrestled free from Thunderbird's grasp and fell down into the ocean with a great splash. The splash was so big that it shook all the waters and even the land. The waters rose up and covered the land. Trees were ripped from the soil, houses were shattered, and many people died before the ocean waters **receded**.

Thunderbird and Killer Whale fought for many days. At last, Killer Whale knew he could not win, and he swam away. Gradually, the fish returned and the people had food again. Ever since, the people have never forgotten how Thunderbird helped them.

According to the story, Thunderbird's wings cause the sound of the thunder. This is common in most Thunderbird myths. But this story seems to explain something else. Many researchers believe this story is about a tsunami, or tidal wave, that struck the Pacific Northwest hundreds of years ago. Tsunamis are caused by earthquakes in the earth's crust, deep beneath the ocean surface. The **vibrations** from the earthquake create waves, and if the earthquake is strong enough, these waves can form a tsunami. Tsunamis are very destructive when they strike land. It is no surprise that the survivors would mark the event with a myth like this.

Chapter 7

Severing Ties

THE BIG QUESTION
How did the arrival of settlers and the U.S. government's actions affect Native Americans living west of the Mississippi River?

Native Americans were well adapted to the cycles and patterns of nature. Whether they lived in a small fishing village or a large, sprawling farming society, they learned to survive in harmony with their surroundings. They used wood from trees, but they did not cut down all the trees. They used every part of the buffalo, but they did not kill all the buffalo. They made jewelry using stone or shell beads and sometimes copper, but they did not destroy the mountains and rivers to get all these materials. They gathered nuts and berries, but not too many, and they always left enough new seeds to sprout for future generations.

The basic rules and patterns of nature never really change. The cycles remain the same. And yet, change is in everything. Change comes with every season, just as it comes in various stages of our lives. These are the changes we understand and know to expect. But sometimes there are other types of changes. Nobody can predict exactly what the future will bring. Native Americans understood this fact long before they encountered Europeans.

Through their myths and spiritual ceremonies, Native Americans gave thanks and praise to nature's helping spirits—the plants, animals, waters, and sunshine. But they also asked the spirits for safety and mercy. They asked to be spared from famine, drought, and war. Most years, the people were happy, well-fed, and at peace with their neighbors. But they knew there would also be **lean** years when the buffalo herds were too thin, or too little rain fell on the corn and bean crops. They knew there would be wars and conflicts with other tribes as well.

Some tribes controlled better land with more food and resources than other tribes. Some tribes grew to be large and dominant, while others simply survived from season to season. Some tribes faced more trials and tribulations than others. Sometimes, one tribe would force another tribe off its land, so, for example, an Eastern Woodland tribe might have to adapt to life on the plains, or a Plateau tribe might have to learn to survive in the desert. Sometimes the victors of war would take the losers captive, or adopt them into their tribe. Other times, mighty tribes fell and weaker ones rose up.

And so everything changed, and yet in many ways everything stayed the same. In spite of all of life's challenges, Native Americans upheld their way of life for thousands of years. Wherever they were, they strived to live in harmony with their surroundings. They lived according to the same patterns and cycles as everything else in nature. When the acorns ripened and fell, then it was time to gather and eat acorns. When the buffalo moved, it was time to move the village. And when the spring rains fell, it was time to plant new seeds. Year after year and generation after generation, according to these cycles, Native American tribes created their own history.

Europeans who migrated to the Americas did not share the same traditions and beliefs as Native Americans. Aside from their culture, religion, and technology, Europeans had different beliefs regarding land ownership and individual rights and liberties. To understand just how very different they were, it is important to reflect on what life was like in Europe.

In the late 1400s, Europe was just emerging from the feudal system of the Middle Ages. Most people were still tied to farming the land, the bulk of which was owned by rich, influential members of the nobility. There was no "free" land to explore and settle on. There was little social mobility. For three hundred years after Columbus's first journey, the exploration and colonization of the "New World" brought incredible new wealth to European nations. However, a large part of that wealth went straight to the same royals and aristocrats who already owned all the land and resources in the "Old World."

Wide-open prairie

Then came the founding of the United States in 1776. This new nation put in place systems of laws designed to protect the right to "life, liberty, and the pursuit of happiness." Now, the New World offered new hope and opportunity for even the most lowly members of European society. The New World offered land, ready to be farmed, to all, including those who would never have had such an opportunity in their own countries.

However, it wasn't quite that simple. By the late 1700s, land in the East had been claimed, and there was stiff competition for jobs. Therefore, many new **immigrants** looked beyond the East to the frontier—the untamed wilderness—for opportunities.

The Nation Doubles in Size

In 1803, President Jefferson completed the Louisiana Purchase, which doubled the new nation's territory. This huge area of land was mostly unmapped and unknown wilderness to Europeans settling in the United States. In 1804, Lewis and Clark began their famous journey to explore the land west of the Mississippi River. Their explorations helped spark interest in this land. By 1850, people realized that all the land—the American West as it came to be known—was not only vast but also full of resources. It did not take long for this news to travel to Europe. For those escaping the troubles of the Old World, the American West seemed like a haven. There, anyone could live free and **prosper** if they were willing to work. Also, as it turned out, they needed to be willing to fight or "manage" the Native Americans who had been living there for thousands of years.

Throughout the second half of the 1800s, immigrants, largely from Europe, flowed into the United States. Many became "pioneers," risking everything for a chance to settle and build new lives. Generally, pioneers were not there to live in harmony with nature or abide by Native American customs and laws. They were there to tame the land and gain wealth from it.

Some of the resources were obvious: endless forests, fine soil and ranch land, massive buffalo herds, and sometimes even gold nuggets just sitting there on the ground waiting to be picked up. But some of the most valuable resources were buried underground, such as coal, iron, oil, copper, and other minerals. These resources did not shine like gold or silver, but over time they proved even more valuable. They provided the raw materials for America's growing cities and industries. For the people of the United States, the American West was a great treasure trove of land and resources. However, Native Americans had already made this land their home.

Captain Meriwether Lewis (1774–1809) and William Clark (1770–1838) on their transcontinental expedition

To the pioneers and the U.S. government, who wanted to settle on this land, the presence of Native Americans was a problem. The U.S. government decided that one way to control and confront Native Americans was to encourage immigrants and other people in crowded eastern cities to move west. This gave rise to one of the most important acts of legislation in U.S. history: the Homestead Act of 1862. With the passage of the Homestead Act, vast **tracts** of land throughout the West were made available to new settlers. Anyone age 21 or older could apply for a homestead of usually 160 acres. In exchange for the land, homesteaders had to live on it for at least five years and improve it by creating a profitable farm or ranch. The Homestead Act triggered a land rush throughout the American West, as thousands of new settlers staked their claims and worked to build new lives.

This painting, *At the Sand Creek Massacre* by Howling Wolf (1874–1875), is part of an important art tradition developed by Plains Indians in the 1800s.

Of course, many of these homesteads were on Native American homelands. Many tribes felt they had no choice but to defend their way of life. Problems usually started with small disagreements, but they soon spiraled out of control. The brutal Sand Creek Massacre of 1864 is an example of this. In that case, U.S. soldiers in the Colorado territory attacked a peaceful village and killed over 100 Cheyenne, mostly women, children, and elderly men. The tribe's warriors were out hunting at the time, but when they returned and saw what the soldiers had done, they swore **revenge**. The surviving Cheyenne and other tribes attacked settlers throughout the area, kidnapping and killing entire families. Thus began a bloody cycle of revenge.

Wars between Native Americans and settlers from the United States broke out in every region of the West, from the Great Plains to California. These wars were bloody and costly. In an effort to end the fighting and solve the "Indian Problem" once and for all, the U.S. government greatly expanded the reservation system. This meant forcing Native Americans onto areas of land set aside for them. This had begun years earlier with the Indian Appropriations Act of 1851. Then, Congress set aside money to create reservations throughout what is now Oklahoma (where the Cherokee were forced to move during the Trail of Tears). Most tribes refused to move onto reservations at first, so the U.S. Army tried to force them. The fighting only increased and the wars became bloodier.

After years of war, some tribes managed to make peace treaties with the U.S. government. Instead of moving to distant reservations, individual tribes were allowed to carve out little land reservations in their ancestral homelands. This was the case with some of the stronger, larger tribes. They still lost much of their freedom and land, but each tribe was treated as an independent nation within the United States.

Unfortunately, none of these peace treaties lasted long. Settlers continued to **encroach** on Native American land anyway. Furthermore, the reservation lands were usually unsuited to supporting the tribes. Due to little rain and poor soil, Native Americans often left the reservations to hunt and gather foods. The main problem, as far as the settlers and the U.S. government were concerned, was that some tribes still had powerful, popular leaders. Even on reservations, Native Americans maintained power and influence because they continued to work together as tribes. The U.S. government felt that the tension and fighting would continue as long as Native American tribes were treated as independent nations within a nation.

With the Indian Appropriations Act of 1871, the United States officially stopped treating each tribe as a separate nation. After 1871, by law, all individual Native Americans were considered "**wards** of the federal government." The U.S. government no longer wished to deal with tribes as a whole. Instead, they wanted to deal with individuals, in the hopes that the tribal structure would finally collapse once and for all. Native Americans were no longer independent, but they were not U.S. citizens, either. In the eyes of the law, they became dependents with few freedoms and rights to do anything unless the government agreed.

Of course, one act of Congress did not change a structure that had been in place for thousands of years. While some Native Americans decided the only way to survive was to lay down their guns and learn to live according to the laws of the United States, many others refused to give up. To them, life on the reservations was no life at all, and they would rather die fighting than watch their families starve. But eventually the U.S. government did succeed in breaking the tribes. Although the Appropriations Act of 1871 did not bring an end to the wars, it did mark the beginning of a particularly tragic chapter in the story of Native American **resistance**.

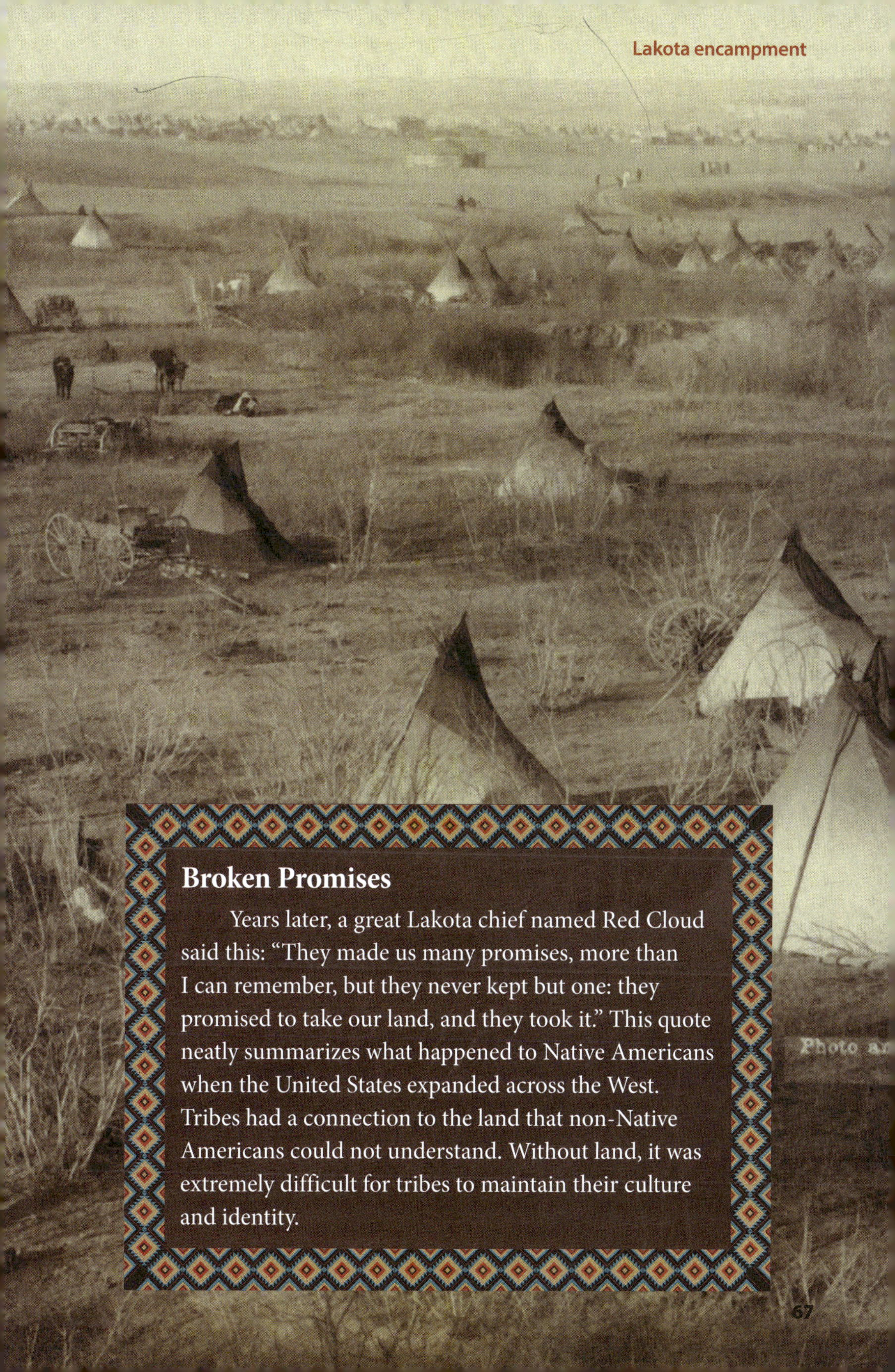

Lakota encampment

Broken Promises

Years later, a great Lakota chief named Red Cloud said this: "They made us many promises, more than I can remember, but they never kept but one: they promised to take our land, and they took it." This quote neatly summarizes what happened to Native Americans when the United States expanded across the West. Tribes had a connection to the land that non-Native Americans could not understand. Without land, it was extremely difficult for tribes to maintain their culture and identity.

Chapter 8

Your Name is Luther

THE BIG QUESTION
How did events in Luther's life affect his view of **assimilation**?

Richard Henry Pratt is not a famous name, but his story does provide an important window into Native American history. Through Pratt's story, we learn that there were people in the United States who did not want to see Native Americans killed off or trapped on poor reservations. Some wanted to help Native Americans assimilate and become part of a rapidly changing nation. In the end, Pratt's efforts did not help in the way he had hoped. This is his story.

Colonel Richard Henry Pratt on horseback

Pratt was not a Native American. He was born to a family of British descent in New York State. In 1850, at age 10, his family moved west to Indiana, which was a frontier state at the time. Needing money, Pratt's father followed the Gold Rush to California. He got lucky and struck gold! Unfortunately, he died before he could bring that gold home.

As a result, at age 13, Pratt was fatherless and penniless. As the oldest child, he had no choice but to leave school and work in order to help provide for the family. He grew up understanding the importance of hard work, as well as the value of knowing a trade or skill that would provide an income. Later, during the Civil War, he volunteered for the Indiana Volunteer **Cavalry** and fought for the Union. He was a good soldier—smart, brave, and hardworking. Pratt liked army life, and he stayed with the cavalry after the war was over. He was assigned to the Tenth Cavalry Regiment, or the "Buffalo Soldiers" as they were known. Their job was to make sure the Lakota and other plains tribes stayed on their reservations.

This was easier said than done. The land on most reservations was very poor, so people could not farm there. The U.S. government promised to provide money, food, fuel, and other supplies to the reservations, but there was never enough for everyone. Many people preferred to die fighting than starve on the reservations. As a result, the Tenth Cavalry was involved in several of many "Indian Wars" between the United States and the Great Plains tribes.

Although Pratt was employed to control and even fight Native Americans, he also saw firsthand how horrible living conditions were on the reservations. He understood why people would rather fight than surrender. Pratt **sympathized** with Native Americans, and he thought there must be a better alternative to war and starvation.

In the army, Pratt had contact with Native American prisoners of war. The army was not sure what to do with these prisoners because they knew that if they released them, they would probably have to fight them again. Pratt tried to figure out how to enable the prisoners to return to a life of peace rather than remain in prison or die in battle. He believed Native Americans needed to be taught how to live according to the laws and customs of the United States. He taught them to speak English, and then he taught them to read and write. What Pratt realized is that Native Americans were just like him. They wanted to be able to take care of their families, their homes, and their land. They wanted food, shelter, and safety. They cared for their children and wanted the best for them. Pratt believed that, in order to have those things, it would be best if Native Americans learned to read and write English and were more familiar with U.S. ways and customs.

Pratt had a favorite saying: "Kill the Indian to save the man." This did not mean that he literally wanted to kill Native Americans. He actually wanted to save their lives, but in order to do that he believed it was necessary to strip away everything that made them Native Americans. His goal was "assimilation through education." As he saw it, Native American culture was the main problem, and the solution to the problem was to replace that culture with something new. To do that, he believed Native Americans needed to change their language, their religious beliefs, all of their habits and customs, and even their clothing and hairstyles. Today, it is no surprise that many people blame Pratt for trying to destroy what was left of Native American culture. In many ways, that is exactly what he wanted to do.

Pratt gathered support for his idea, and eventually he convinced Congress to give him some money to open an **experimental** school. The U.S. Army agreed to let him use an old barracks in Carlisle, Pennsylvania. Pratt converted the buildings there into the Carlisle Indian Industrial School. At this school, Native Americans would learn to speak, read, and write in English. They would also learn about U.S. history and customs, such as Thanksgiving and the Fourth of July. They would no longer be allowed to dress like Native Americans and were instead made to wear uniforms. They would not be allowed to sing, dance, or tell their old stories, either. They would be taught to cast aside their ancient ways and learn a new way to live in America.

Native American children reading at the Carlisle School

To find students for his new school, Pratt went back to the same reservation lands where he once fought as a soldier, in South Dakota and Nebraska. He talked to some of the tribal leaders. He told them he had an idea to help their children find a bright, happy future. This brings us to the story of another colorful, fascinating character in American history: Luther Standing Bear.

Luther's Story

When Luther was born, he was named Plenty Kill, because his parents thought he had the heart of a hunter and warrior. He was born in the Black Hills of South Dakota in 1868. Back then, many Lakota and other Sioux tribes were still at war with the U.S. Army. Plenty Kill lived on a reservation,

Native American children studying anatomy at the Carlisle School

but he was raised according to the old, traditional ways. He learned to hunt buffalo and ride a horse. He also learned to fight. Plenty Kill's father was a great warrior. He called the U.S. soldiers "Long Knives," because of the swords carried by cavalry officers like Richard Henry Pratt.

When Plenty Kill was a boy, his father made a bow and arrows for him. The bow and all the arrows were painted red as a sign that his father had been wounded in battle. Plenty Kill grew up expecting that he, too, would someday fight and possibly die in battle against the Long Knives. However, his father did not really want his son to become a warrior. Like many other Lakota, he was tired of fighting. Instead, he wanted something different for his son.

Then, one day, Richard Henry Pratt came to talk to them about the Carlisle School. Pratt took Plenty Kill's father and other tribal elders to visit the new school. On the trip, they also went to New York City and Washington, D.C. They met the president of the United States, the "Grandfather of the Long Knives." When Plenty Kill's father returned from his trip, he said this:

> *"My son, since I have seen all those cities, and the way the Long Knife people are doing, I begin to realize that our lands and our [animals] are all gone. There is nothing but the Long Knives everywhere I went,*

and they keep coming like flies. So we will have to learn their ways, in order that we may be able to live with them. You will have to learn all you can, and I will see that your brothers and sisters follow in the path that you are making for them. Someday I want to hear you speak like these Long Knife people, and work like them."

So, Plenty Kill went to Carlisle, Pennsylvania, along with 146 other Native American children, mostly from Great Plains tribes. There, he chose his new first name—*Luther*—at random from a list of names on the chalkboard. He could not yet read, but the teacher ordered him to choose a name anyway, and *Luther* was the one he chose.

Life at the Carlisle School was totally different than anything Plenty Kill, now Luther, had ever known, and it certainly was not much fun. The teachers forced all the boys to cut their hair, which is something Lakota men never did. The boys were very angry about it and did not understand, but they had no choice. Discipline at the school was strict and punishments were severe. If the boys refused, they were punished, and then they had to get a haircut anyway.

Native American children digging for potatoes

After their haircuts, the children received new clothing. They had never worn such tight, scratchy garments and they were very uncomfortable. Aside from the sadness of separation from their families, the worst part was that they were not allowed to speak their own language. The children were only allowed to speak English, which was impossible at first since none of them knew that language. Luther was a very fast learner, though, and he grew to enjoy reading and writing.

Luther was a star student at Carlisle and became a recruiter for the school, meaning that he encouraged other Native Americans to send their children there. The people at the U.S. Bureau of Indian Affairs liked what they saw at the Carlisle School. They built about 25 more "Indian boarding schools" around the country, all modeled after the Carlisle School and

Native American children learning to read and write at the Carlisle School

funded by the government. They also encouraged church missions and other organizations to create similar schools on reservations.

Unfortunately, few Native American children were as successful as Luther and other members of the first class at the Carlisle School. Most boarding schools were run like military bases, and children were often treated very badly. In some schools, children were treated more like enslaved workers than students. They lived in poor conditions and diseases were widespread. If they tried to run away, they were captured and forced to do physical work as punishment. Pratt himself complained that the schools were hurting rather than helping Native Americans. Eventually, he complained so much that he was fired from the Carlisle School. He continued to promote "assimilation through education," but he was never very successful, and the schools never improved much. Many were closed by the late 1920s.

Luther went on to live a full and fascinating life. Despite efforts by Pratt and the teachers at the Carlisle School, Luther never forgot his native language and customs. He never cut his hair again, either, and he did not think any other Native Americans should have to. Luther spent the rest of his life working to preserve Lakota **heritage**. He wrote books and gave speeches, and he even became a movie actor. He tried to make sure Hollywood film directors portrayed Native Americans in a fair, honest way, instead of always presenting them as villains or savages.

Luther believed in the importance of education, and he was always grateful to Pratt for the chance to attend his school. However, Luther did not agree that Native Americans should abandon their culture. He thought Lakota children should learn about Lakota history and that they should be proud of their culture and beliefs. Today, Luther Standing Bear would be happy to see that present-day Native Americans are proud of their heritage and have not abandoned their culture.

Chapter 9

Battle of the Little Bighorn

THE BIG QUESTION
Why was the Battle of the Little Bighorn important in the shared history of the European settlers and Native Americans?

In previous chapters you read about **conflict** between Native Americans and settlers moving west. This is the story of the Battle of the Little Bighorn. It is an event that stands out in the history of this conflict.

Lieutenant Charles Varnum was awake long before **reveille** that morning. In fact, he had not slept at all the night before, and he was not alone, for there was going to be a battle that day, and everyone knew it. He watched the sunrise and light fog drifting across the wide prairies of southern Montana. This was a pleasant place to be in the summertime, even if you had to wear a heavy wool uniform like Varnum and his fellow cavalrymen.

The troops were camped in a little river valley. The day before, Varnum had noticed silvery rainbow trout in the nearby creek, and perhaps the thought had crossed his mind that it would be nice to spend the day fishing beside that little creek. However, Varnum knew very well that this day would hold no time for leisure or relaxation. They were at war, and the enemy was near. In fact, according to his scouts, the enemy was just on the other side of that river.

The war became known as the Black Hills War, because much of the fighting was in or around the Black Hills of South Dakota. Later, it was also referred to as the Great Sioux War of 1876. Lieutenant Varnum was in the Seventh Cavalry Regiment, commanded by Lieutenant Colonel George Armstrong Custer. This was only one of many "Indian Wars" and other bloody conflicts between Native Americans and U.S. forces.

As Chief of Scouts, Lieutenant Varnum gathered intelligence, or important information, about the enemy's location and strength. Varnum had a tough, ragtag group of men under his command. The scouts included warriors from the Arikara and Crow tribes. Their people once fought the U.S. soldiers, too, but they had surrendered and moved onto the reservations. Their tracking skills and knowledge of other tribes was very useful.

The day before, June 25, Varnum sent his scouts to explore the banks of the Little Bighorn River. They reported finding a very large Lakota Sioux village. They said there were many warriors in the village, but they did not know how many exactly. They only knew that it was a very big village with hundreds of tipis. As was his duty, Varnum reported this information to Custer, his commander.

Little Bighorn River, Montana

Custer wanted to see the village, so Varnum and his scouts took him to the top of the tallest nearby hill. From there, they could see smoke from the campfires, and they could see a few tipis and some horses, but not much else. Custer said he wanted to attack the village, but the Arikara and Crow scouts protested, saying they had never seen such a large village. Nonetheless, Custer saw this as an opportunity to deal a major blow to the enemy and maybe even end the war, so he ordered his men to prepare for an attack.

General George A. Custer, 1876

Years earlier, during the Civil War, Custer had gained a reputation for being fearless and aggressive. However, he also had a reputation for being **reckless**, taking big risks with the lives of his soldiers. Ten years later, Custer was still the same type of soldier. Like everyone else in the Seventh Cavalry, Varnum had great respect for Custer and was proud to serve under his command. Still, Varnum could not help feeling that maybe, this time, Custer was being too reckless.

Custer could not see the whole village from the top of that hill because it extended several miles along the river valley. He only saw the very edge of the village. Beyond that, there were at least 10,000 Lakota Sioux camped along the river, including as many as 2,000 warriors. And the Lakota were not alone. Their **allies**, the Arapahoe and Cheyenne, were there, as well. In the past, the tribes had often gathered in this valley of the Little Bighorn River because it was good hunting ground and there was plenty of water nearby. In 1876, with war raging all around, they were all gathered in this place. Amongst the thousands gathered together were a famous Lakota holy man named Sitting Bull, along with a great warrior-chief named Crazy Horse.

Many members of the Lakota had tried to live on the reservations. They had signed treaties with the federal government. The treaties said it was their land and nobody else's. But settlers moved in anyway, and the reservations

Sitting Bull was a Lakota holy man.

kept getting smaller and smaller. At last, the Lakota left the reservations. They packed up their tipis and traveled across the plains into Wyoming and Montana to hunt buffalo and live free. Of course, the U.S. government wanted them to go back to the reservations. They told the Lakota to return by midnight on January 31, 1876, or there would be war. The Lakota did not return to the reservations, and the Black Hills War started the next day.

Sitting Bull was a famous spiritual leader, known among all the Lakota and their allies. He told his people to have courage in their war against the *Wasichu.* That is what the Lakota called the soldiers and settlers: *Wasichu.* The true meaning of this word is not certain, though some have concluded that it means "person who takes the fat," or someone who is greedy. Anxious and uncertain of their future, the tribes gathered in this valley in the early summer of 1876, because Sitting Bull was going to perform a Sun Dance. The Sun Dance was an ancient, sacred ritual. During the Sun Dance, Sitting Bull prayed for a vision of the future. He asked the spirits what would happen to his people. Sitting Bull predicted that the Lakota would win a great victory in battle.

Sitting Bull was not the only important leader in the great village on the Little Bighorn that day. Crazy Horse was there, as well. In some ways, Crazy Horse was a little like Custer, bold and reckless. In battle, he rode straight at the enemy, but no arrow or bullet ever found him. All the warriors were happy to follow Crazy Horse wherever he went, because he always found victory.

Chief Crazy Horse

After talking with Varnum and his scouts, Custer ordered his troops to prepare to attack the village. Custer planned a surprise attack, but he soon realized this was impossible. After all, the Lakota had scouts, too, and it is not easy to hide a cavalry regiment for very long out on the plains.

The regiment had 11 companies, each with around 50 or 60 men. Custer divided the regiment into three brigades, or groups of companies. He sent three companies with Captain Benteen and another three companies with Major Reno. Custer kept the largest force of five companies, totaling 210 men, under his direct command. At first, Lieutenant Varnum was a little disappointed when he learned that he was going with Reno's force. Varnum wanted to ride with Custer and the main force.

Prior to the Battle of the Little Bighorn, one of Custer's assignments had been to map this area to locate a suitable site for a future military post. During the expedition, geologists discovered gold. This discovery caused an invasion of miners and others to the Black Hills in violation of the treaty of 1868.

Custer did take several of Varnum's scouts because he needed them to guide him to the village. The Arikara and Crow had long been enemies of the Lakota, since the days before any Europeans knew about America. Therefore, Varnum's scouts were willing to go and fight with Custer. However, as he was riding out with Reno's troops, Varnum saw his scouts preparing for battle. They were singing their death songs, which meant they did not expect to survive the day.

Custer took his brigade to the north along the right bank of the Little Bighorn River, looking for a good place to cross and attack the village. Reno crossed over to the left bank, and his troops moved north on that side of the river. Soon, scouts were reporting that the Lakota knew the soldiers were coming and they were not running away. Custer sent a messenger to Reno and ordered him to attack the village and force the Lakota to come out and fight. Custer, meanwhile, was a mile or so upriver, and he planned to attack at the same time, creating **chaos** and confusion in the village.

Reno's brigade dismounted from their horses and approached a few tipis on the edge of the village. They moved forward in a line, cautiously, with the troops up front and the officers, including Lieutenant Varnum, to the rear. As they approached the village, Varnum saw children running away. Several women mounted horses and they were the first ones to ride out and shoot at the soldiers. Then the warriors arrived. At first, there were only a few. They hid in the tall grass and fired their guns from a distance.

Reno's soldiers and the Lakota shot back and forth for about 20 minutes. One of Reno's men was wounded during this time, but that was all. However, Lieutenant Varnum was a trained and experienced scout, which means he had good eyes and a good sense of what was happening around him. He realized that the Lakota warriors were gathering behind a nearby hill. Varnum sent a scout to see, and sure enough, he reported that there were at least 500 warriors there. Before Varnum could warn Reno, the warriors rode their horses around from behind the hill.

The ground shook and the air filled with their war cries as warriors swarmed toward Reno's brigade. Bullets and arrows whizzed all around, and then the soldiers began to fall. Panic and fear spread through Reno's brigade

***Opening of the Battle of the Little Bighorn* by Amos Bad Heart Bull (1869–1913)**

as they realized they were outnumbered. Reno also panicked. He ordered his men to mount their horses, but then he ordered them to dismount, and then to mount again. At last, he simply ordered everyone to retreat, and they all ran or rode away as fast as they could. They reached the top of a hill, but the Lakota were everywhere. That might have been the end of Reno and all his men, except Captain Bennett's brigade happened to appear at just the right moment. Today, that hill is called Reno's Hill. Reno and Bennett stayed on that hill the rest of that day, all night, and into the next day. All the while, they expected Custer and his men to ride to the rescue at any moment.

Custer never made it across the Little Bighorn River. He tried, but before he and his men were halfway across, all the rest of the warriors from that huge village came out to meet them. The only survivors of that fight, the only ones who lived to tell the story of "Custer's Last Stand," were Native American warriors. Custer and every one of his men died that day.

As to what exactly happened to Custer, there are different stories. Most seem to agree on a few details, though. The Lakota attacked Custer and his men as they crossed the river. Many of his men died there in the water. The rest probably broke into smaller groups of 20 or 30 men. Most of the fighting was over within a few minutes. Custer and some of his men probably made it to the top of a small hill. There they may have formed a circle and fought a little while longer before being totally overrun.

After Custer was dead, all the warriors went back and attacked Reno and Benteen and their men. They fought all the rest of the day and into the night. The fighting began again the next morning, but the Lakota learned that more army soldiers were coming. Soon after, the Lakota broke camp and scattered across the plains once again, and the war continued. Sitting Bull's prediction was correct. Crazy Horse and the Lakota warriors did win a great victory that day. It was their last great victory. Less than a year later, in May of 1877, after many more battles, Crazy Horse and the last of his warriors finally surrendered to the *Wasichu.*

As for Lieutenant Varnum, he remained in the cavalry for many years and continued to fight the few remaining Lakota and other people who dared to resist. In 1890, he won the nation's highest military award, the Medal of Honor, for his actions fighting the Sioux one last time near a place called Wounded Knee.

Retreat of Major Reno's Command **by Amos Bad Heart Bull (1869–1913)**

Chapter 10

The Taking of the Land

THE BIG QUESTION
How did the Dawes Act change Native Americans' land rights?

Henry Laurens Dawes (1816–1903)

By the late 1880s, nearly all Native Americans had been forced onto reservations or assimilated into U.S. society. Forcing people onto reservations did not bring peace. Even on the reservations, far away from their ancestral lands, stripped of their culture and forced to learn a new way of life, some Native Americans would not give up the fight.

Eventually, Congress passed the Dawes Act (officially the General Allotment Act of 1887). The Dawes Act was the final act that forced an end to the conflict between the United States and Native American tribes. This act "did away with" reservations altogether, based on the belief that the only path to survival for Native Americans was for them to assimilate and own land as individual family farmers. It did not simply take more land or carve up existing reservations, the Dawes Act actually aimed to destroy the heart of Native American cultural identity, the one thing no other treaty or act of Congress had done.

Under the Dawes Act, reservations were broken up and Native American families who lived on those former reservations received 160 acres of land, the same amount granted to settlers, or homesteaders, by the Homestead Act. This act forced Native Americans to work and survive as individuals and not as part of a tribe. However, most of the acreage that was allocated was on existing reservation land that was usually unsuitable for growing crops. While most homesteaders had a good chance of making a living off their 160 acres, most Native Americans had no such luck on their dry, dusty allotments. Any land not claimed by Native Americans was made available for sale to non-Native American settlers. Those who could not earn a living from their allotment had to sell their land to non-Native American settlers for needed cash. The former reservation homelands were chopped up into many little pieces and hunting and fishing territory was lost. Many people left the former reservation land and never returned. Those who remained struggled to survive. Worst of all, rather than a sense of belonging to the land, they felt a sense of **isolation** and sadness. The people were scattered and all that remained—it seemed—were stories and memories.

To understand why the Dawes Act was so damaging to Native American tribes, you must understand what lay at the heart of Native American cultural identity. Many factors contribute to cultural identity. Language, clothing, food, and religious practices are all important, but they are really only pieces of the puzzle. These things only provide clues to a person's culture. The true core of a person's cultural identity cannot necessarily be seen, heard, or tasted. Cultural identity is something people feel and know deep down inside, regardless of what they wear or do and regardless of where they live.

When Native American children went off to the boarding schools (such as the Carlisle Indian Industrial School), they changed their clothing and language. They traded in their homemade animal-skin clothes for wool suits and dresses. They learned to speak English. They learned about a new religion, and they learned how to work in factories and on farms. They did everything their teachers told them to do—everything that was supposed to erase their cultural identity. But it did not work. In the end, they were still Native Americans.

Why? What was it about the cultural identity of Native Americans that could not be easily erased or forgotten? The answer to this question is both simple and complicated: land. It is simple because it is easy to see why the land was so important to Native Americans. But it is complicated because, according to Native American traditions, there is more to land than dirt and rock. There is more to it than plants, animals, and all the resources necessary for survival. Land is not simply a place where a tribe lives. Land is part of the tribe itself. Land is the thing that makes the tribe whole.

Anyone can learn to hunt, but how many people know how to make a perfect bow and arrows using only materials available on the grassy prairies? How many people can look at the forest floor and immediately know what kinds of animals have walked through the area in the past few days, how big they were, and in which direction they were headed? How many can predict the weather by watching birds or observing the moon? How many people do you know who can find enough food in the desert to feed an entire extended family of 50 or more people? To not only survive but also to raise a family and live comfortably in the forest, plains, or desert requires great skill and knowledge, more than a single person could teach himself or herself. Living such a lifestyle brings people into direct and intimate contact with nature, with the land itself, as well as with the sky and waters and with other people with whom they must work and share in order to live.

This was very different from the way people of European descent lived at the time, and it is very different from the way Americans and Europeans live today. Rather than conquering or taming the land, Native Americans blended into the land. They built sturdy, cozy houses. They moved across the land, following age-old trails. They had excellent tools, but not machinery or factories. They possessed incredible amounts of knowledge—knowledge not necessarily found in a library.

For people living today, survival in the forest or other wilderness would require all our energy and time. How much spare time would you have for fun and games if you found yourself in the wild, with nothing but your hands and brain to provide food, clothing, housing, and fuel? Most likely, you would spend all day looking for food and still go to bed hungry, and probably cold, too. Not so for Native Americans. Native Americans lived comfortably and usually had plenty to eat. They had time for things other than hunting and gathering. They made music and danced and told long, engaging stories. They had celebrations and feasts, and they played games. They were skilled artisans, crafting boats, fine pottery, basketry, jewelry, dolls, headdresses, baby cradles, and all sorts of beautiful objects using whatever was available on the land. This was true long ago, and it is still true today.

From this closeness and intimacy with nature, Native Americans developed their truest sense of cultural identity. Their knowledge of the land was the source not only of food and shelter but also of their stories and beliefs. The spirits they worshipped lived on the same land as everything else. Furthermore, wherever they went, Native Americans walked in the footsteps of their ancestors, whose very flesh and blood was also part of the land. For Native Americans, *everything* was connected to the land. As long as a tribe was together on the land, they were able to cling to their cultural identity. Without land, there could be no tribe.

And so, after decades of wars, treaties, and acts of Congress, the U.S. government finally understood that any land Native Americans were permitted to own as a tribe allowed them to maintain their cultural identity. This is where the Dawes Act finally succeeded where other acts and treaties had failed. It destroyed the sense of connection between the tribes and the land. In the process, it almost defeated the tribes themselves.

Before the Dawes Act of 1887, there were nearly 150 million acres of land in Native American hands. By 1934, when the Dawes Act was finally overturned, Native Americans owned only 48 million acres. In other words, as a whole, Native Americans had lost over two-thirds of their land. Fortunately, though, with the overturning of the Dawes Act and the Indian New Deal of 1934, Native American tribes were allowed to own land once again. Furthermore, they were allowed to exist as separate nations within the United States. Today, the total land owned by Native American tribes has risen slightly, to about 55 million acres. That is only about 2 percent of the total land in the United States, but it was enough for Native American tribes to **revive** and renew the core of their cultural identities—the connection to the land on which the tribe depends. That revival continues to this day, nearly 100 years later.

The Dawes Act

The most important part of the Dawes Act involved the division, or allotment, of land to individual owners. As long as the Dawes Act was in effect, no tribe was allowed to claim ownership of any land. Instead, the land was divided into individual lots and given to individual owners.

Besides the destruction of their cultural identity, Native Americans also lost even more land as a result of the Dawes Act. Many simply sold their land to anyone who was willing to buy it. Others lost their allotments because they went into debt after borrowing money to try to make ends meet. Some allotments were never given to Native Americans at all but simply handed over to homesteaders.

Hopi Petition

In March of 1894, the Hopi people in the Arizona Territory sent a **petition** to "the Washington Chiefs" in response to the Dawes Act of 1887. They had observed U.S. Agents marking their land and were worried about the effect the Dawes Act would have on their way of life. Thomas Keam, owner of a trading post, transcribed the Hopi petition.

> *"During the last two years strangers have looked over our land with spy-glasses and made marks upon it, and we know but little of what this means. As we believe you have no wish to disturb our possessions, we want to tell you something about this Hopi land.*
>
> *None of us were asked that it should be measured into separate lots and given to individuals for this would cause confusion."*

The Hopi's land was arid and a difficult place to grow crops and, over hundreds of years, they had learned to adapt to the environment.

> *"...our fields are numerous but small, and several belonging to the same family may be close together, or they may be miles apart, because arable localities are not continuous."*

They shared farmland among families and moved their farms when winds blew the fertile sands across the land.

> *"The American is our elder brother and in everything he can teach us, except in the method of growing corn in the waterless sandy valleys, and in that we are sure we can teach him."*

They did not want to lose their cooperative way of life or the freedom to move their farms as needed.

> *"We most earnestly desire to have one continuous boundary ring enclosing all the Hopi lands, and that it shall be large enough to afford* ***sustenance*** *for our increasing flocks and herds."*

The Bureau of Indian Affairs never sent a response to the petition.

Moqui Villages
Arizona March 27/28 1894

To the Washington Chiefs:

During the last two years strangers have looked over our lands with spy-glasses and made marks upon it, and we know but little of what this means. As we believe that you have no wish to disturb our possessions, we want to tell you something about this Hopi land.

None of us were asked that it should be measured into separate lots, and given to individuals for this would cause confusion.

The family, the dwelling house and the field are inseparable, because the woman is the heart of these, and they rest with her. Among us the family traces its kin from the mother, hence all its possessions are hers. The man builds the house but the woman is the owner, because she repairs and preserves it; the man cultivates the field, but he renders its harvests into the woman's keeping, because upon her it rests to prepare the food, and the surplus of stores for barter depends upon her thrift.

A man plants the fields of his wife, and the fields assigned to the children she bears, and informally he calls them his, although in fact they are not. Even of the field which he inherits

he U.S. government continued to carve up Hopi land. However, several years later, they gave up due to ontinued resistance and confusion about land rights.

Chapter 11

The Ghost Dance

THE BIG QUESTION
Why did the U.S. government fear the Lakota's cultural connection to the past, and how did this affect the way they dealt with the Lakota people?

Wounded Knee Creek is a narrow, minor trickle on the great Pine Ridge Reservation in South Dakota. If not for the events of December 29, 1890, this creek would not be known beyond the Black Hills. Because of that day, however, that little creek is remembered as the site of the Wounded Knee **Massacre**.

Chief Red Cloud

Why was there a massacre at Wounded Knee Creek? There is no good answer or reason, other than the fact that the creek was near the home of Red Cloud, a Lakota chief and the most important resident of the Pine Ridge reservation. Red Cloud and his warriors fought against the United States for many years. He even had his own war named after him: Red Cloud's War (1866–68). He did not win Red Cloud's War, but he did not lose, either. In the end, he signed a peace treaty and agreed to live on the reservation. After his war, Red Cloud always tried to keep peace with the United States. He did not join Sitting Bull and Crazy Horse in the Great Sioux War. He was not there at the Battle of the Little Bighorn when Custer and all his soldiers were killed. Even so, Red Cloud was always respected as a great warrior. He never went to battle again, but he continued to fight for his people's rights.

Red Cloud was both a warrior and a peacemaker. Of course, he would have preferred to live free on the plains with his horses, hunting buffalo and carrying on the ancient traditions. He understood why so many other Sioux did not want to assimilate. He understood why they were angry and why they

Standing Bear, Chief of the Sioux

would rather fight, even though they knew they could not win. Still, he tried to convince others that peace was better than war, and survival was better than dying. Like his good friend Luther Standing Bear, Red Cloud believed the Lakota and other Native Americans needed to accept that they were part of the United States rather than continue fighting it.

Red Cloud was almost 70 years old when the Dawes Act of 1887 was passed. Like all the other acts and treaties, the Dawes Act took land from the tribes, but it took more than that. In reality, the Dawes Act was an effort to destroy the tribes themselves. Most of Red Cloud's old friends were long gone by then, but there was a new generation of Lakota growing up on Pine Ridge and other reservations, and he was worried for their future.

Red Cloud's people struggled to survive on the poor, isolated reservation lands. They were supposed to give up their ancient customs and raise crops on their allotments, but this was all much easier said than done. The Bureau of Indian Affairs (or BIA, an agency of the federal government) sent them some supplies and teachers to help start their farms. Unfortunately, the reservation lands were too hot and dry for farming, and the Lakota could not grow enough food. The BIA agents decided the crops failed because the Lakota were too lazy. Instead of giving them more money and food to help them survive, the BIA gave them *less* with the hopes that this would motivate them to work harder. But, you cannot grow crops in poor soil with no rain, no matter how hard you work.

As Red Cloud and other leaders were trying to figure out how to guide their people into the future, a new form of hope was slowly taking shape. It started in Nevada, on the reservation of the Northern Paiute people, a Great Basin tribe. One day, during a solar eclipse, a spiritual leader, or shaman, named Wovoka had a vision. In his vision, he saw his ancestors living happily according to the ancient ways. Wovoka claimed that the Creator spoke to him and gave him a message for his people. The message was that they should love and care for one another and learn to live in peace with everyone. If they did this, according to Wovoka's vision, then the people would be **reunited** with their ancestors.

In his vision, Wovoka also saw a special dance, called the Ghost Dance. He was supposed to teach this dance to his people, and this would help them reconnect with their ancestors. Wovoka showed his people how to do the Ghost Dance, and they showed other tribes. For people who had lost so much, the Ghost Dance offered new hope. Word of Wovoka's vision spread beyond the Great Basin and across the Great Plains. According to some rumors, the Ghost Dance would return the world to the way it was before Europeans ever set foot on the land.

Some Lakota spiritual leaders traveled from their reservations in South Dakota to Nevada. They met with Wovoka and learned more about his vision and the Ghost Dance. Perhaps these leaders believed that the Ghost Dance would magically return life to the way it was before the "white men" arrived. More likely, they simply saw the Ghost Dance as a way to revive their people's

Ghost dance of the Sioux Indians

confidence and spirits. If nothing else, the Ghost Dance provided a connection to the past, to better days. The Lakota leaders returned to the reservations in South Dakota and taught the rest of the Lakota about the dance.

However, the U.S. government did not want the Lakota to reconnect with their past. They wanted them to work as farmers on the reservations and live according to U.S. laws. On one reservation, called Standing Rock, the Ghost Dance was especially popular. The BIA agents there were nervous that the Ghost Dance was a sign that the Lakota were planning to start a new war. The BIA agents called for help from the Seventh Cavalry, Custer's old regiment, and they moved in to try to put a stop to the Ghost Dance once and for all. This created great tension on the reservation, and rumors spread that the Seventh Cavalry was planning to kill everyone involved with the Ghost Dance.

Chief Spotted Elk

Many Lakota people were afraid, and they left Standing Rock reservation. They fled to another nearby reservation and joined with Chief Spotted Elk and about 100 of his warriors. The BIA agents already considered Spotted Elk to be a troublemaker, and he figured they would come for him next. Spotted Elk knew there was only one safe place to go: Pine Ridge, home of Chief Red Cloud, the peacemaker. If anyone could help calm tensions and bring peace, it was Red Cloud.

About 350 men, women, and children set off with Spotted Elk toward Pine Ridge. They carried white flags as they walked, to show that they wanted to make peace. It was a long journey, and Spotted Elk was an old man. Along the way, he got sick with pneumonia. On December 28, 1890, the Seventh Cavalry intercepted Spotted Elk and his people before they reached Pine Ridge. Sick and exhausted, Spotted Elk surrendered peacefully. It was freezing cold outside, like any winter day in South Dakota, and snow was starting to fall. The soldiers escorted Spotted Elk and his people to a campsite on the banks of Wounded Knee Creek while they figured out what to do next.

Men, women, and children set off for Pine Ridge.

Even though Spotted Elk was sick and most of the people in his group were women and children, the soldiers were still afraid the Lakota might try to cause trouble. That night, as the Lakota rested at Wounded Knee Creek, the Seventh Cavalry surrounded the camp and set up four Hotchkiss guns on nearby hills. Each Hotchkiss gun looked like a little cannon, but it had five revolving barrels, so it could fire bullets very rapidly, much like a modern machine gun.

The next morning, December 29, soldiers moved into the camp and demanded that the Lakota surrender all their weapons. There were only about 100 or so warriors in the group, and they were surrounded by nearly 500 cavalry. They were not happy, but most Lakota realized that they had no choice and handed over their guns. Others had no weapons at all. However, a few refused to surrender their weapons. They argued with the soldiers, and someone fired a shot. To this day, nobody knows for sure who fired that first shot. It might have been an accident. It really does not matter, though, because there is no doubt as to what happened next. As soon as that first shot rang out, all the soldiers opened fire, not only with their rifles, but also with the powerful Hotchkiss guns. Some Lakota warriors tried to fight back, but most were killed before they had a chance. The fight was done in a matter of minutes. Really, it was not a fight at all; it was a massacre. When it was all over, at least 250 Lakota men, women, and children were dead, including Spotted Elk. Some estimates run as high as 300, but it is impossible to know for sure.

The Wounded Knee Massacre is remembered as the final fight of the Sioux nation, even though it really was not much of a fight. It **symbolizes** the end of nearly 400 years of armed conflict between Native Americans and the powers of Europe and the United States. But you already know this was not really the end. In fact, history shows that Wounded Knee was, in certain ways, a new beginning. Many years would pass, but gradually Native American tribes reclaimed their cultural heritage and their status as America's First Nations. We cannot change the past, but we can seek the truth about what really happened. We can show respect for the lands and rights of the First Nations. Every American should feel a responsibility to help ensure that Native American cultural heritage is protected for future generations.

The Navajo Code Talkers

The Second World War (1939–45) was the bloodiest and most destructive war in human history. Worldwide, the war claimed tens of millions of lives and left major cities throughout Europe and Asia in ruins. America's cities were spared, but not its soldiers. Nearly 300,000 Americans were killed in battle, and more than twice that many were wounded. Many Native American warriors are counted among those dead and wounded U.S. soldiers.

At least 25,000 reservation-born Native Americans served in the U.S. armed forces during the Second World War. Hundreds of them served as Code Talkers. In many ways, Code Talkers were just like millions of other Americans who served their nation during the war. They went into battle and faced all the same dangers as any other soldiers. However, a Code Talker's main job was not to fight like most other frontline soldiers. The Code Talker's job was to talk, in his native language, to other Code Talkers.

For a young Navajo or other Native American, it was not necessarily an easy thing to decide to serve and fight for the U.S. armed forces. Some Native Americans were against the war and were not eager for their young men to go off and fight in it. It is not hard to understand why some felt this way. Wounded Knee and other **atrocities** were still fresh in many memories. The elders spoke of how the government soldiers, the "Long Knives," killed women, children, and old men. They saw these terrible events with their own eyes. Many were still angry and bitter. So why would a young Navajo volunteer to fight for the United States? For many, the answer was actually quite simple: because the United States had become their nation.

Navajo code radio talkers of 1st U.S. Marine Division, World War II, 1944

As citizens, they were duty-bound to support and defend that nation, and so they did. In 1924, all Native Americans officially became citizens of the United States. With the rights and privileges of citizenship come certain responsibilities and duties. During wartime, the government can **draft** citizens into the military. During the Second World War, all eligible men aged 18 to 45 could be drafted into the armed forces. As citizens, Native American men were eligible for the draft just like other men.

Many did not wait to be drafted, though. Around the country, millions of Americans were eager and proud to volunteer to fight for their country. From the reservations, twice as many Native Americans volunteered as were drafted. In other words, of those 25,000 Native Americans who fought in the war, the majority volunteered, and they were proud to do so.

Aside from courage, the Navajo Code Talkers' most important trait was also the core of their identity: their language. This was the same language they were punished for using at the Indian boarding schools. There, the teachers made them learn English so they could survive and prosper in the culture and society of the United States. But before they went away to those schools, they grew up with Navajo traditions and language. In their hearts and minds, they knew the world according to Navajo words, and they never forgot them. Who could have guessed that, one day, the United States itself would depend on those same Navajo words for its very survival!

For an army at war, communication is as important as weapons or supplies. To fight and win, an army must have weapons, food, and good communication. Before radios, soldiers had to stay close to their commanders, as they did during the Civil War, when troops marched in line, shoulder-to-shoulder. They did this so they could hear their officers' orders. Other than shouting, the only way for frontline soldiers without a radio to communicate with other units was by messengers on foot or on horseback. Armies during the Civil War and after also had the telegraph, which was kind of like the telephone, but it required miles of cable and was not useful in the heat of battle.

Navajo code radio talkers in the jungle during World War II

The Second World War was different. Radio and telephone communication allowed armies to spread out and operate in smaller units. As long as they had radios, soldiers could communicate and coordinate with each other whether they were a hundred yards or a hundred miles apart. Radios were absolutely essential on every battlefield during the Second World War, whether on land, at sea, or in the air.

Just as importantly, information transmitted by radio needed to be secure, so enemy forces could not intercept it and use the information to their advantage. The problem with radios is that the enemy can always listen in if they tune to the same radio frequency. Therefore, radio operators communicated using complex codes, so the enemy could not understand. Unfortunately, that led to the need to create codes that could not be cracked by the enemy.

All armies used radios during the Second World War, and all armies developed radio codes. Therefore, all sides were engaged in creating, protecting, and cracking secret radio codes. They could not simply say in plain language what they were doing and planning, because then the enemy would know exactly what they were going to do. In fact, the Allies were able to break Axis codes during the Second World War, and the Germans and Japanese did not even realize it at first. This enabled the Allies to learn where Axis forces planned to send their troops, making it easier for Allied troops to **foil** Axis plans. By contrast, the Germans and Japanese were only able to break *some* Allied codes, but they never broke the Navajo code. Nobody even came close. That is because there was something special about the Navajo language itself.

The traditional, ancestral home of the Navajo people is in the Four Corners region of the United States, where the borders of Colorado, Utah, New Mexico, and Arizona meet. The Navajo language is related to the language of the nearby Apache people, as well as to some northwestern tribes all the way up in Canada and Alaska. (These languages belong to the Athabaskan language family.) Generally, however, Navajo is unlike most other languages. In fact, it is considered to be one of the most difficult languages for **nonnative** speakers to learn.

Basically, the only way to truly learn Navajo is to grow up hearing it every day, so that your understanding of the world is based on the unique rhythms and sounds of the language. For those born into that culture, the language was and remains central to Navajo identity. The Navajo people can always learn to talk to the outside world using English, Spanish, French, Mandarin, Japanese, or any other language, but the Navajo language is really theirs and theirs alone.

When the U.S. Marines learned about the unique qualities of the Navajo language, they decided to recruit a special, top-secret group of soldiers from the reservations. The first Navajo Code Talkers completed basic training in June, 1942, months after the surprise attack on Pearl Harbor. Then they went to a special school at Fort Elliot, in California, where they learned communication skills and, most importantly, they developed and mastered their special code. Initially, 29 young men completed training and became the first Navajo Code Talkers.

By early 1943, they were in combat, moving from island to island in the Pacific with the other U.S. Marines. Ultimately, Navajo Code Talkers took part in the bloodiest and most important battles in the Pacific war, including Guadalcanal, Tarawa, and Iwo Jima. By the end of the war, nearly 400 Navajo warriors served as Code Talkers. At least 11 were killed in action during the war, including one of the original 29, and many more were wounded.

Combat in the Pacific islands was brutal and savage. The U.S. Marines fought over every inch of terrain, from sandy beaches through dense jungles and up and down countless hills and mountains. The Code Talkers were there on every battlefield, passing vital information up and down the chain of command. As long as the Code Talkers were alive and their radios worked, they provided the vital communication link the Marines needed in order to win.

Of course, the enemy was always listening, trying to break the Navajo code. Japanese spies listened endlessly, day and night, but they could never make any sense of what they heard. The thing about Navajo is that individual sounds, or phonemes, are difficult to identify, as if certain sounds are hidden from nonnative ears. Navajo is a highly descriptive language. Basically, Navajo words involve more sounds than words in other languages. When spoken,

Navajo code radio talkers receiving and transmitting information

the individual sounds and syllables flow like a rushing river from the native Navajo tongue. If you pick apart a Navajo sentence and compare it to its English translation, you usually find that Navajo uses many more individual syllables to express what appears in English as a simple phrase or sentence. As just one example, the single English word *ammunition* is *beh-eli-doh-be-cah-ali-tas-ai* in Navajo. When spoken, many of those individual sounds are hidden from the nonnative ear. When spoken along with many other words, it is nearly impossible for a non-Navajo listener to understand where one word ends and another begins, much less what any of it means.

Eventually, the Japanese did figure out that the Code Talkers were speaking Navajo, but that did not bring them any closer to breaking the code. The only way they could possibly hope to break the code was to capture a Navajo and force him to translate it for them. However, knowing how to speak Navajo was only the first step toward understanding the code.

A Soldier's Story

One Navajo soldier named Joe Kieyoomia learned that understanding Navajo could be dangerous.

Joe was born and raised on a Navajo reservation in New Mexico. He decided as a child, long before the war started, that he wanted to be a U.S. soldier. When he was old enough, he joined the New Mexico National Guard. So he was already in the army when the war broke out. Back then, the Pacific nation of the Philippines was owned by the United States, so there were U.S. naval and other military bases there. Joe was stationed on a base in the Philippines when Pearl Harbor was attacked. Shortly after that, Japanese forces invaded and conquered the Philippines. Like thousands of other American soldiers early in the war, Joe was forced to surrender, and he became a Japanese prisoner of war.

It is important to understand that the U.S. Armed Forces were racially segregated during the Second World War. Almost all the U.S. soldiers the Japanese encountered were Caucasian, or white-skinned. Most Japanese had never seen a Native American. When the Japanese soldiers first saw Joe, they actually thought he was a Japanese soldier. They accused him of being a **traitor** and punished him. Eventually they believed his story that he was actually a Native American.

Once they learned he was Navajo, they realized he might be able to break the Navajo code. But Joe had never heard of the Navajo code. He was just a regular soldier. Although he was a native Navajo speaker, nobody ever told him about the code. The Japanese forced Joe to listen to recordings of the Code Talkers. He listened and he told the truth: he understood the Navajo words, but he still could not understand the code. He could not help them—and they were not pleased!

Because there were no Navajo words for things like *artillery* and *airplanes*, the Code Talkers assigned other words. A tank was a tortoise. A bomb was an egg. A fighter plane was a hummingbird. That all made sense to the trained Code Talkers, but to Joe, the coded messages sounded like nonsense. That is exactly what it was supposed to sound like to an untrained ear.

Eventually the Japanese gave up. It was obvious Joe did not understand the code. Joe survived the war, but just barely. His captors eventually moved him to the Japanese homeland shortly before war's end. They put him in a basement prison in a city called Nagasaki. As it happened, this was the second and final city onto which the United States dropped an atomic bomb. Japan finally surrendered the next day, and the war was over. Amazingly, Joe survived Nagasaki. He returned home to the Navajo Nation and lived to be an old man.

Back home on the reservation, Joe became friends with his fellow Navajo war veterans. Many of them served as Code Talkers, and they felt sorry for Joe when he told them about his experiences. He told them he never would have shared their code with the Japanese, even if he could break it. When he asked them how their code worked, though, the Code Talkers would not talk about it. They were all sworn to secrecy, and in fact not one of them ever said a word until the program was declassified in 1969. Until then, most Americans did not even know the Navajo Code Talkers existed, except the many Marines who fought alongside them.

Finally, in 1997—over 50 years after the end of the war—the U.S. Congress officially thanked the remaining Navajo veterans for their service as Code Talkers. Without them, Congress acknowledged, history might have turned out very differently.

World War II

Many countries were involved in the Second World War, but they all fought for one or the other of two sides: the Axis Powers and the Allies. The Axis Powers included primarily Germany, Japan, and Italy. The Allies included the United States, Britain, France, the Soviet Union (Russia), Australia, and many other smaller countries in Europe and Asia.

Enrichment

Ancestors' Words

Great Granny told all the grandchildren to gather around her rocking chair for a story. The children loved to hear stories, and they were always polite and eager listeners, but this time they were confused when Great Granny spoke. They could not understand a single word of her story. Finally the youngest put his hand on her knee and said, "Excuse me, Great Granny, but we can't understand what you are saying."

Great Granny's old, sun-worn face crinkled and she said in a stern voice, "Listen, child. Of course I know you do not understand, but that is only because you have not listened. Now, listen."

She continued her story, using the same language, which the children still did not understand. As they listened, however, they realized that they had in fact heard this language before. Although they did not understand it, they still recognized it. It was already in their minds, faint but familiar, like the memory of a dream. Their hearts warmed just to hear the words of the ancestors echoing in Great Granny's story.

Afterward, she explained the meaning of her story in the language the children could understand. She told them it was a story of her own creation, about a language only she and a few other people on earth still knew how to speak. She explained that once, hundreds of years before, that language echoed over the low hills and shallow valleys of the Great Plains. But there were fewer speakers every year. Now, some 90 years after her birth, Great Granny was one of the last.

This is the story she told them:

Of all the plants Mother Nature made when the earth was young, there is one unlike any other. It has roots and branches, just like other plants. Like other plants, it has seeds, which fall from the branches and sprout into new plants.

This plant—the last one Mother Nature made—is not used for food or medicine. It does not give wood for houses or fibers for basket-weaving. It is not like any of those other plants. Still, this plant nourishes all the people and animals. Families, villages, and entire nations depend on this plant. Even the animals must have it. None could exist without it!

This plant can live thousands of years, longer than the oldest sequoia or redwood, and yet this plant is not something you see or touch. You hear it. You can hear it now. It is language. Language is the last plant Mother Nature made. All you children, you are like seeds on the language plant. This language I speak to you now, it is the language of your ancestors. It is already inside you, ready to grow if you will let it.

The children enjoyed hearing the story, but the younger ones did not really understand it. They grew restless and were eager to go back outside to play. However, the oldest one, Dorrie, knew there was an important lesson in Great Granny's story. She stayed by the rocking chair for a while to hear more. "Great Granny, I want to learn that language," Dorrie said. "Can you teach me?"

Great Granny said, "Yes, I can teach you, but it will not be as easy for you as it was for me. You see, when I was a girl, this language filled the air around me, so that I learned without even trying. I am sorry it will never be that way again."

"But the language is still alive, isn't it, Great Granny?" asked Dorrie.

"Yes, it is alive. But it is like a potted plant now. It can only grow and spread so much, and only with great care," Granny replied.

Dorrie visited her Great Granny as often as she could. She learned to name things in nature: the grasses, wind, trees, rivers, and prairie dogs. She learned about medicinal herbs and about the spirit of the buffalo. She learned to talk about the weather and the stars. Once, when she was older, the whole family gathered for a reunion. Dorrie was thrilled to meet the few elderly cousins and aunts and uncles who also spoke the old language and have them all in one place! That day, the words of the ancestors filled the air, and when she closed her eyes, Dorrie imagined she was in a little tipi village on the Great Plains, perhaps after a successful hunt, when everyone was happy and hopeful and full of laughter.

After the party, a heavy sadness settled on Dorrie's heart, because she was afraid it was the last time she would ever hear that sound. Rather than wallow in sadness and regret, she felt inspired to learn all she could about her native language. More importantly, she wanted to preserve it, so future generations could hear it as well. To Dorrie, that ancient language was a potted plant, and she was the caretaker. Like a plant, the language required tender care and upkeep. If she left it alone for too long, it would wither and die.

Later, when she went off to college, Dorrie discovered linguistics, the scientific study of language. She enrolled in a linguistics class about Native American languages. Dorrie learned that linguists have identified about 56 different Native American language families. (That's only in North America; there are many more in South America.) Like a family tree, each language family has branches. Each branch is related, but not identical, to the main branch. Dorrie learned that the language Great Granny taught her belongs to the Caddoan language family. The Caddoan family has five branches, or separate languages: Wichita, Caddo, Kitsai, Arikara, and Pawnee. This family dates back at least 3,000 years and is native to areas of the central and southern Great Plains region.

Languages within a family are similar in some ways, but they are not the same. If, for example, a Pawnee speaker met a Wichita speaker, they would not be able to understand each other right away, even though each speaks a Caddoan language. European languages belong to families, as well. Spanish, French, and Italian are Romance languages. All Romance languages share similar grammar and vocabulary. By contrast, English and German are not Romance languages. They belong to a different family altogether. Therefore, a native Spanish speaker usually finds it easier to learn French than English. In the same way, Wichita is related to Pawnee, but they are not the same language any more than Spanish and French are the same. Still, a Wichita speaker could learn Pawnee more easily than he or she could learn a language from a different family, like Navajo.

Dorrie also learned that the Caddoan language family is almost totally dead, or moribund, as linguists prefer to say. Of the five Caddoan languages, one—Kitsai—is already extinct. That means there are no more speakers, native or otherwise. Once it is extinct, it is almost impossible to revitalize a language, or bring it back to life, even if it exists in written form or audio recordings. Once a language is extinct, only the linguists really know or care that it ever existed.

One day, Dorrie told her linguistics professor about her Great Granny's language. She told him about the "potted plant" that she was trying to preserve and grow. "That is a fascinating story," the professor told her. "But do you know there are hundreds of other young people like you all over the United States carrying similar seeds and potted plants?"

Dorrie was not surprised to hear this, actually, because she knew there were once hundreds of different languages in the Americas. She also knew many of those languages were almost moribund, if not totally extinct. The professor told Dorrie to go to the library and do some research so she could learn what all the other linguists had already learned. After all, linguists have studied the ancient Native American languages for a long time. In the library, Dorrie found books about Native American linguistics dating back 100 years or more.

Of the 56 Native American language families, most are very small and contain only one or two languages and have a handful of speakers, if any. Many are extinct. However, some are alive and well. Navajo, a member of the Athabaskan family, has at least 150,000 speakers, more than any other. At least nine Native American language families are relatively healthy, meaning some of the languages in those families are spoken by hundreds if not thousands of people.

Still, every one of those families has individual languages that are extinct or dying. For example, the Athabaskan family includes not only Navajo but also Plains Apache, which is extinct. A little over a century ago, both Navajo and Apache were common on the plains. What happened to Apache? Why did that language die while Navajo lives on? Why have so many Native American languages disappeared, and how can the rest of them be saved? Dorrie found some answers to these questions as she continued her linguistics research.

It was obvious to her why so many languages like Kitsai and Apache were already extinct. The process began when the Europeans decided to settle and expand, moving across the land. Expansion went hand-in-hand with war and the spread of diseases that devastated Native American populations. Finally, the forced resettlement onto reservations and the boarding school experience sealed the fate of many Native Americans and their culture. Entire tribes vanished, along with most aspects of their culture and heritage. Others scattered or gathered in small numbers on dusty reservations. Off the reservation, the ancient languages did not seem to have much value. With each passing generation, fewer and fewer children learned the words or had any use for them.

By the time she graduated college, Dorrie felt more like a gardener than a mere caretaker. She knew how to grow and nurture the seed. She was excited to learn about many people throughout the United States dedicated to preserving Native American languages and culture.

Dorrie learned that there are three basic ways to preserve a language: writing, recording, and speaking. Prior to European contact, Native Americans did not have written languages. All their languages—along with their knowledge and traditions—were passed from generation to generation by word-of-mouth. Some early European explorers and missionaries learned native languages and **transcribed** them into written formats. Since then, linguists have continued developing written versions of various languages, including Navajo. Written records certainly make it easier to preserve the vocabulary and grammar of a language, but that alone is not enough to keep the language alive.

During the 1900s, new technologies enabled linguists to record Native American voices. Today, many of those recordings are still available (in libraries and on the Internet), so people can hear native speakers. But a recording is only a sample, more like a little song or echo of the past than anything else. By themselves, recordings cannot preserve or revitalize a language.

Writings and recordings can help, but the only way to truly keep a language alive is to use it. A language is only useful if more than one person can speak it, though, so the most important goal is to share and teach others. Dorrie graduated from college just in time to join a new generation of young language gardeners determined to save their ancestral languages. She worked to preserve and grow the four remaining Caddoan languages.

Today, there is only one Wichita speaker. Pawnee has the most with about 25 speakers. The other two fall somewhere in between. Most of the remaining native speakers are elderly, but not all of them. Some younger ones, like Dorrie, are still learning and talking and filling the air with the ancestors' words. Without people like Dorrie and her fellow linguists, the Caddoan languages, along with many others, would be gone, vanished like the buffalo from the prairie.

Glossary

A

ally, ***n.*** a supporter; a person or group who helps another person or group toward a common goal (**allies**)

assimilation, ***n.*** the process of becoming part of a society or culture (***v.*** **assimilate**)

atrocity, ***n.*** a horrific, awful, or cruel event (**atrocities**)

B

band, ***n.*** a group of people, animals, or things that act together to achieve a common purpose (**bands**)

birthright, ***n.*** a right someone has because he or she was born into a specific group or family, or because it is a right of all people belonging to that group

C

cavalry, ***n.*** a part of an army made up of soldiers on horseback

chaos, ***n.*** complete confusion or disorder

conflict, ***n.*** a war or a battle that is part of a larger war

council, ***n.*** a group of people chosen to lead or give advice

custom, ***n.*** a tradition or behavior that is common among a group or family; a ritual (**customs**)

D

distinct, ***adj.*** being different in a noticeable way

draft, ***v.*** to require people to join the military, usually during wartime (**drafted**; ***n.*** **draft**)

E

encroach, ***v.*** to gradually take something away from someone else

experimental, ***adj.*** using a new, different, or unproven way of thinking or doing something

F

foil, ***v.*** to prevent someone from doing something or achieving a goal

forced relocation, ***n.*** the act of making people move to a new place against their will

H

harpoon, ***n.*** a long spear used to hunt large fish (**harpoons**)

heritage, ***n.*** the traditions and beliefs that are unique to a specific group and handed down from generation to generation

I

identity, ***n.*** the characteristics that make a person or group different from other people or groups

immigrant, ***n.*** someone who leaves his or her own country to live in another country (**immigrants**)

immunity, ***n.*** the body's ability to resist or fight off a disease

indigenous, ***adj.*** originating in a certain location or region

isolation, ***n.*** a separation from other things or people

L

lean, ***adj.*** having few resources, such as food, fuel, and money

loincloth, ***n.*** a piece of cloth worn around the hips as clothing by men in certain cultures, usually in warm climates

M

massacre, ***n.*** the killing of a large number of people or animals

meek, ***adj.*** quiet; gentle

N

nimble, ***adj.*** able to move quickly and gracefully

nonnative, ***adj.*** not originally from a specific place or country

P

petition, ***n.*** a written request, signed by many people, asking someone in power to do something

property deed, ***n.*** an official piece of paper that shows who legally owns a piece of property (**property deeds**)

property line, ***n.*** the boundary, or border, that indicates where one piece of property ends and another begins (**property lines**)

prosper, ***v.*** to become rich and successful; to flourish

Q

quiver, ***n.*** a bag or case used to carry arrows

R

recede, ***v.*** to move back from; withdraw (**receded**)

reckless, ***adj.*** careless; acting without considering the consequences

remnant, ***n.*** a leftover piece; a small part of the whole (**remnants**)

reservation, ***n.*** a separate area of land in the United States set aside for Native Americans to live on (**reservations**)

resistance, ***n.*** refusal to accept something; being against something

reunite, ***v.*** to bring back together after a separation (**reunited**)

reveille, ***n.*** an early morning bugle or drum call signaling soldiers to report to duty

revenge, ***n.*** the act of doing something to hurt someone because they did something to hurt you

revive, ***v.*** to make someone or something strong, active, alive, or healthy again (***n.*** **revival**)

S

scout, **1.** ***n.*** someone who is sent somewhere in advance of others to gather information; **2.** ***v.*** to observe someone or something in order to gather and report information about that person or thing

supplement, ***v.*** to add or contribute another section or part to make something else complete

sustain, ***v.*** to keep alive

sustenance, ***n.*** food and drink that gives nourishment and keeps someone or something alive

symbolize, ***v.*** to represent, or be a symbol of, something (**symbolizes**)

sympathize, ***v.*** to feel or express concern or support for someone or something (**sympathized**)

T

tan, ***v.*** to change animal skin into leather using a special process (**tanning**)

tension, ***n.*** discomfort felt when different people or groups disagree and feel anger toward each other; a strain (**tensions**)

toll, ***n.*** the cost in health or life

tract, ***n.*** an area or strip of land (**tracts**)

traitor, ***n.*** someone who betrays his or her side or switches loyalties, particularly in a war

transcribe, ***v.*** to write down; to make a written record of oral speech (**transcribed**)

transition, ***n.*** a change

V

vibration, ***n.*** a continuous, fast, shaking movement (**vibrations**)

vision, ***n.*** something that you imagine or dream

W

wakan, ***n.*** in the Sioux culture, a supernatural power

ward, ***n.*** someone who is under the care or control of the government (**wards**)

Writer

Mike Ford

Expert Reviewer

Jeffery L. Hantman

Illustration and Photo Credits

A New Land and Water Map of the Entire Earth, 1630 (coloured engraving), Hondius, Henricus (1597-1651) / Private Collection / Bridgeman Images: 6–7

age fotostock / age fotostock / SuperStock: 30–31

Apache Girl 1903 (photo) / Universal History Archive/UIG / Bridgeman Images: Cover/i/1

At the Sand Creek Massacre, 1874-75 (pen, ink & w/c on ledger paper), Howling Wolf (1849-1927) / Allen Memorial Art Museum, Oberlin College, Ohio, USA / Gift of Mrs. Jacob D. Cox / Bridgeman Images: 64–65

Avi Katz: 52, 53, 54, 55, 56–57

Blend Images / Blend Images / SuperStock: 12–13

Buyenlarge / Buyenlarge / SuperStock: 66–67

Captain Meriweather Lewis (1774-1809) and William Clark (1770-1838) on their trans-continental expedition from the Missouri to the Pacific Ocean in 1804-06 (oil on canvas), Burnham, Thomas Mickell (1818-66) / Private Collection / Bridgeman Images: 62–63

Carlisle Indian School (Anatomy Class): Library of Congress, Prints & Photographs Division, LC-USZ62-72449: 71

Carlisle Indian School (Digging): Library of Congress, Prints & Photographs Division, LC-USZ62-55420: 72

Carlisle Indian School (Writing Class): Library of Congress, Prints & Photographs Division, LC-USZ62-55422: 73

Carlisle: Library of Congress, Prints & Photographs Division, LC-USZ62-71002: 70

Cherokee Indians are forced from their homelands during the 1830s, 1993 (colour litho), Tauss, Herbert (1929-2001) / National Geographic Creative / Bridgeman Images: 10–11

Chief Crazy Horse, Oglala Sioux / Private Collection / J. T. Vintage / Bridgeman Images: 77b

Chief Spotted Elk, 1899 (oil on canvas), Burbank, Elbridge Ayer (1858-1949) / Butler Institute of American Art, Youngstown, OH, USA / Museum Purchase 1912 / Bridgeman Images: 94a

Col. Richard Henry Pratt on horseback: Library of Congress, Prints & Photographs Division, LC-USZ62-26798: 68

Construction of a tule shelter--lake Pomo 1924 (photo) / Universal History Archive/ UIG / Bridgeman Images: 36

Cooking acorns 1924 (photo) / Universal History Archive/UIG / Bridgeman Images: 36–37

Core Knowledge Staff: 67, 88

Courtesy of The Bancroft Library, University of California, Berkeley, Call Number: ISHI--POR7: 32

Custer's Last Stand, English School, (20th century) / Private Collection / © Look and Learn / Bridgeman Images: 78

Dustin Mackay: 8, 14–15, 16, 18, 19, 20, 94b

Fancy Collection / Fancy Collection / SuperStock: 33a

Flirt / Flirt / SuperStock: 44–45

FogStock LLC / FogStock LLC / SuperStock: 42–43

General George A. Custer, 1876 (b/w photo), Barry, David Frances (1854-1934) / Private Collection / Peter Newark American Pictures / Bridgeman Images: 76

Hemis.fr / Hemis.fr / SuperStock: 51

Henry Laurens Dawes (1816-1903), US Senator, photo by Nowell, Pittsfield, Massachusetts (albumen photo), American Photographer, (19th century) / American Antiquarian Society, Worcester, Massachusetts, USA / Bridgeman Images: 82

Interfoto / Interfoto / SuperStock: 9

Joseph Ma: 22–23, 24, 25, 27, 28

JTB Photo / JTB Photo / SuperStock: 60–61

Library of Congress, Prints & Photographs Division, LC-USZ62-52423: 92–93

Life on White / Life on White / SuperStock: 17

Lina Liberace: 4–5

Makah Indian whalers landing whales at Neah Bay, Washington 1911 (photo) / Universal History Archive/UIG / Bridgeman Images: 45

Marka / Marka / SuperStock: 74–75

Martin Hargreaves: 34, 35a, 35b, 38–39, 48–49, 49a, 49b, 49c, 50

Minden Pictures / Minden Pictures / SuperStock: 21

Navajo code radio talkers of 1st US Marine Division, 1944 (b/w photo), American Photographer, (20th century) / Private Collection / Peter Newark Pictures / Bridgeman Images: 97

Northwest coast of American Indians, family life, 2007 (w/c on paper), Harlin, Greg (b.1957) / Private Collection / Wood Ronsaville Harlin, Inc. USA / Bridgeman Images: 47

Opening of the Battle of the Little Big Horn (ink on paper), Amos Bad Heart Buffalo (1869-1913) / Private Collection / The Stapleton Collection / Bridgeman Images: 80

PhotoAlto / PhotoAlto / SuperStock: 58–59

Red Cloud, Dakota Chief, wearing a headdress, 1880s (b/w photo), Barry, David Frances (1854-1934) / Denver Public Library, Western History Collection / Bridgeman Images: 90

Retreat of Major Marcus Reno's command (ink on paper), Amos Bad Heart Buffalo (1869-1913) / Private Collection / The Stapleton Collection / Bridgeman Images: 81

Sarah Darnell / Sarah Darnell / SuperStock: 33b

Sioux Indians hunting buffalo, 1835 (oil on canvas), Catlin, George (1796-1872) / Private Collection / Peter Newark American Pictures / Bridgeman Images: 84–85

Sitting Bull (b/w photo), American Photographer, (19th century) / Private Collection / Ken Welsh / Bridgeman Images: 77a

SoFood / SoFood / SuperStock: 33c

Standing Bear, Chief of the Sioux, wearing ceremonial robes and full length head-dress of eagle feathers: Dakota, North American Plains Indians. Photograph c1885-1890. / Universal History Archive/UIG / Bridgeman Images: 91

Stock Connection / Stock Connection / SuperStock: 41

The U.S. National Archives and Records Administration, NARA Identifier: 300340; Creator(s): Department of the Interior, Office of Indian Affairs. (1849 - 09/17/1947), from Series : Letters Received, compiled 1881 - 1907. HMS Entry Number(s): PI-163 91, Record Group 75, Records of the Bureau of Indian Affairs, 1793–1999.: 89

Totem pole (painted wood), American School / Horniman Museum, London, UK / Photo © Heini Schneebeli / Bridgeman Images: 46

Tyler Olson / Tyler Olson / SuperStock: 2–3

US NAVY/SCIENCE PHOTO LIBRARY: 98, 101

Core Knowledge Language Arts
Amplify.

Editorial Staff

Susan Lambert, Vice President, CKLA

Julie Weintraub, Senior Account Manager

Elizabeth Wade, PhD, Managing Curriculum Developer

Patricia Erno, Managing Curriculum Developer

Jamie Raade, Senior Curriculum Developer

Amber McWilliams, ELL Specialist

Christina Cox, Copy Editor

Julia Cantuaria, Associate Marketing Manager

Project Management

Matthew Ely, Director of Operations

Jennifer Skelley, Senior Producer

Leslie Johnson, Associate Project Manager

Design and Graphics Staff

Todd Rawson, Design Director

Julia Sverchuk, Creative Director

Erin O'Donnell, Senior Designer

Contributors

Ann Andrew, Desirée Beach, Leslie Beach, Brian Black, Stephanie Cooper, Tim Chi Ly, Nicole Crook, Stephen Currie, Kira Dykema, Carol Emerson, Jennifer Flewelling, Mairin Genova, Marc Goldsmith, Christina Gonzalez Vega, Stephanie Hamilton, Brooke Hudson, Carrie Hughes, Sara Hunt, Rowena Hymer, Jason Jacobs, Leslie Johnson, Annah Kessler, Debra Levitt, Bridget Looney, Christina Martinez, Sarah McClurg, Julie McGeorge, Evelyn Norman, Chris O'Flaherty, Cesar Parra, Leighann Pennington, Heather Perry, Tim Quiroz, Maureen Richel, Jessica Richardson, Carol Ronka, Laura Seal, Cynthia Shields, John Starr, Carmela Stricklett, Alison Tepper, Karen Venditti, Carri Waloven, Michelle Warner, Rachel Wolf

Center for
Early Reading
Amplify.

Core Knowledge Language Arts

Core Knowledge Foundation

Series Editor-in-Chief

E. D. Hirsch Jr.

President

Linda Bevilacqua

Editorial Staff

Mick Anderson
Robin Blackshire
Laura Drummond
Emma Earnst
Lucinda Ewing
Sara Hunt
Rosie McCormick
Cynthia Peng
Liz Pettit
Tonya Ronayne
Deborah Samley
Kate Stephenson
Elizabeth Wafler
James Walsh
Sarah Zelinke

Design and Graphics Staff

Kelsie Harman
Liz Loewenstein
Bridget Moriarty
Lauren Pack

Consulting Project Management Services

ScribeConcepts.com

Additional Consulting Services

Erin Kist
Carolyn Pinkerton
Scott Ritchie
Kelina Summers

Acknowledgments

These materials are the result of the work, advice, and encouragement of numerous individuals over many years. Some of those singled out here already know the depth of our gratitude; others may be surprised to find themselves thanked publicly for help they gave quietly and generously for the sake of the enterprise alone. To helpers named and unnamed we are deeply grateful.

Contributors to Earlier Versions of These Materials

Susan B. Albaugh, Kazuko Ashizawa, Kim Berrall, Ang Blanchette, Nancy Braier, Maggie Buchanan, Paula Coyner, Kathryn M. Cummings, Michelle De Groot, Michael Donegan, Diana Espinal, Mary E. Forbes, Michael L. Ford, Sue Fulton, Carolyn Gosse, Dorrit Green, Liza Greene, Ted Hirsch, Danielle Knecht, James K. Lee, Matt Leech, Diane Henry Leipzig, Robin Luecke, Martha G. Mack, Liana Mahoney, Isabel McLean, Steve Morrison, Juliane K. Munson, Elizabeth B. Rasmussen, Ellen Sadler, Rachael L. Shaw, Sivan B. Sherman, Diane Auger Smith, Laura Tortorelli, Khara Turnbull, Miriam E. Vidaver, Michelle L. Warner, Catherine S. Whittington, Jeannette A. Williams.

We would like to extend special recognition to Program Directors Matthew Davis and Souzanne Wright, who were instrumental in the early development of this program.

Schools

We are truly grateful to the teachers, students, and administrators of the following schools for their willingness to field-test these materials and for their invaluable advice: Capitol View Elementary, Challenge Foundation Academy (IN), Community Academy Public Charter School, Lake Lure Classical Academy, Lepanto Elementary School, New Holland Core Knowledge Academy, Paramount School of Excellence, Pioneer Challenge Foundation Academy, PS 26R (the Carteret School), PS 30X (Wilton School), PS 50X (Clara Barton School), PS 96Q, PS 102X (Joseph O. Loretan), PS 104Q (the Bays Water), PS 214K (Michael Friedsam), PS 223Q (Lyndon B. Johnson School), PS 308K (Clara Cardwell), PS 333Q (Goldie Maple Academy), Sequoyah Elementary School, South Shore Charter Public School, Spartanburg Charter School, Steed Elementary School, Thomas Jefferson Classical Academy, Three Oaks Elementary, West Manor Elementary.

And a special thanks to the CKLA Pilot Coordinators, Anita Henderson, Yasmin Lugo-Hernandez, and Susan Smith, whose suggestions and day-to-day support to teachers using these materials in their classrooms were critical.

Core Knowledge®